THE HUMPTY DUMPTY EFFECT

Brandon M. Bowmar

For Edith*

Proverbs 31:10

Song of Songs 4:1-2

*Edith is a nickname for my wonderful wife.

TABLE OF CONTENTS

WORDS TO KNOW 1

INTRODUCTION 5

CHAPTER 1: THE HUMPTY DUMPTY EFFECT 9

CHAPTER 2: THE "APPLE" IN GENESIS 3 23

CHAPTER 3: THE SERPENT AS SATAN IN GENESIS 3 35

CHAPTER 4: THE RELATIONSHIP BETWEEN DAVID AND JONATHAN 65

CHAPTER 5: THE MAGI AND THE NATIVITY SCENE 83

CHAPTER 6: THE RAPTURE 121

CONCLUSION 152

APPENDIX: THE TROUBLE WITH THE INFANCY NARRATIVES 157

ACKNOWLEDGEMENTS 162

BIBLIOGRAPHY 163

FINAL NOTES 171

WORDS TO KNOW

Biblical study words to impress your friends (and your pastor):

Apocrypha: Deriving from the Greek language, the word literally means "secret" or "hidden." Apocrypha usually refers to a collection of texts that were once part of the Greek Old Testament (Septuagint) but were not considered as canon by the early Church. There are instances where Apocrypha may refer to a New Testament Apocrypha (rather than Old Testament) but that is rarer. It's best to follow the common usage which refers to the collection of texts found in the Septuagint. These texts were written between 200 BC and 100 AD. Examples include 1 & 2 Esdras, Tobit, Judith, and my personal favorite, Bel and the Dragon (sounds like a more interesting version of Beauty and the Beast).

Since it was part of the original Vulgate, the Apocrypha is found in Roman Catholic Bibles and for them is considered canonical. Protestants do not view it as canonical. The adjectival term "apocryphal" may refer to something in the Apocrypha or a story of uncertain origin that is not true. For instance, the story of Isaac Newton discovering the law of gravity after he was hit on the head by an apple is apocryphal (he did notice an apple fall, but he was never hit in the head).

Canon: Literally meaning "rule" or "law," canon refers to the collected sacred texts that the Church views as authoritative. The word has a long-standing and consistent etymological history.

Hebrew: קָנֶה/qaneh—cane or reed.

Greek: κανών/kanon—ruler, standard.

Latin: Canon—Norm, list.

You usually hear talk about canon in two contexts: the Holy Scriptures or a popular fictional story. With the latter, you may hear people argue about whether or not certain characters or ideas are in the established canon. The Star Wars series has produced many extra movies, shows, books, ideas (did Greedo or Han shoot first?), and fan fiction. There is an established canon on what is true to the official storyline and what lies beyond it.

What is important here is the canon of the Holy Scriptures. These are the collection of books that the Church views as authoritative and true. For Protestants, it is the 66 books we typically find in our Bibles. For Roman Catholics and the Eastern Orthodox Church, there are extra books from the Apocrypha added.

Hermeneutics: The science or art of interpretation. The word derives from the Greek word ἑρμηνεύω/herméneuó, meaning to explain or interpret. Hermeneutics focuses on properly interpreting a text. In this book, the focus is on biblical hermeneutics. To speak of someone's hermeneutic is to address their particular method or approach to interpreting the Bible.

Pseudepigrapha: Literally meaning "false writings" or "falsely attributed writings," Pseudepigrapha refers to a collection of texts that are penned as if coming from a person of the Bible but was not actually written by that person. Classification of these texts is difficult as some outliers were composed later (one of these will be explored later in the book by the magi…) but generally they are dated 200 BC to 250 AD.

No pseudepigraphical texts are in the canon.

Septuagint: The earliest Greek translation of the Old Testament (which was mostly written originally in Hebrew). The word derives from the Latin word for seventy. Legend has it that the translation was done by 70 (or 72) Jewish scholars. The majority of Old Testament quotations in the New Testament are from the Septuagint.

You may see it referred to as LXX—Roman Numerals for 70. In a few years, we will have Super Bowl LXX. Can I trademark the name "Septuagint Super Bowl?" Probably not, but I am going to start promoting it…

P.S. Don't sue me, Roger Goodell.

Tanakh: An acronym denoting the Hebrew Bible, which has the same books of the Old Testament for Protestant Christians. Tanakh is formed from the three genres found in the Hebrew Bible: Torah (first five books of the Bible), Nevi'im (the prophets), and Ketuvim (writings). There are two obvious differences between the Tanakh and the Old Testament. First, while the Christian Old Testament divides some books (like 1 and 2 Samuel), the Tanakh holds them as one book (just Samuel). Second, the order of the books is different.

Vulgate: The Latin translation of the Bible that was penned around 400 AD. It was completed by Saint Jerome, and it was the most widely used Bible in Europe for about a millennium. In 1546, the Council of Trent declared the Vulgate to be the official Bible translation for the Roman Catholic Church.

WORD FUN!

Find the "words to know" in this word search.
Please only do this if you own the book.
It's not nice to write in other people's books.

Apocrypha, Canon, Hermeneutics, Pseudepigrapha,
Septuagint, Tanakh, Vulgate

INTRODUCTION

I had always thought it would be neat to write a book, but I never had any specific topic or title in mind. For a few years, my friend and I had jokingly talked about creating a book that was the opposite of a "how to" book. Our inspired book was going to be titled *How Not to do Ministry: Comedic Relief for Those in Ordained Ministry*. By no means am I the world's greatest pastor. In fact, I have made plenty of mistakes,[1] and these mistakes have paved the way for being a better pastor.[2] Having learned some ways not to do ministry and thinking up many creative/quirky things with my cohort in mischievousness, we thought it would be funny to share some ways not lead to a church, preach, teach Sunday School, etc.

For a variety of reasons this book never materialized. After being in school for 21 years straight, the idea of more writing was far from appealing. After finishing seminary, I never wanted to pick up a nonfiction book unless it was for sermon preparation. I had had my fill of reading and writing. After this reprieve from studies, my desire to read and learn returned. My mind began to concoct this idea for a paper on Bible interpretation based on the idea of the Humpty Dumpty poem. I played with the idea in my mind for at least a couple years—thinking about the concept and wondering how I could write about it. Eventually, I made the choice to sit down and start on it. Diving into research, surveys, and writing, I realized that this would be too long for a paper—it would need to be a book. The end result is what you are now reading.

---

[1] Just ask my wife. She can give you the list. ☺

[2] I feel as if I could write a memoir about all the crazy things that have occurred while I have been in ministry. Some of these things include being stuck at the summit of a landfill, being stuck on the roof of a house, figuring out how to properly dispose of a church steeple without having to pay $60 to dispose of it at said landfill, and catching squirrels in a house using a trap with hot dogs as bait. Add to these pastoring during a pandemic and I can teach a bunch of brand-new seminary classes.

One of the beautiful things about this book is that it is completely my own. This writing was not commissioned by a publishing house or a church denomination. This is not part of a doctoral thesis or for any other advanced degree.[3] It was born out of a desire to write something to encourage Christian believers to dive deeper into the Bible and to understand it to the best of their ability. **Thus, my purpose for this book is to get people to read the Word of God and truly know it.** Although the Bible is generally available to all persons in developed countries, biblical literacy is still lacking. People have come to rely more on nonprint media and widely known interpretations of biblical narratives rather than reading the Word of God for themselves.[4] Put another way, too many people are relying on secondhand or thirdhand interpretations of the Bible rather than knowing it for themselves. Like the old game of telephone, where people whisper a message from one person to another around the room, the original content often gets distorted (I do confess to having intentionally changed the message in this game before).

As an introductory example, consider the universally known story of Noah's Ark from Genesis 6-9. Everyone "knows" that Noah brought two of every animal into the ark. The Text does give that specific instruction to Noah in Genesis 6:19. Yet, fewer people know that this is clarified in 7:2-3 to state that seven pairs of every clean animal are to be brought into the ark, but only one pair of unclean animals. Many more would know this if the actual biblical Text were read rather than relying on abbreviated retellings of the story.

The Content of the Book

The book contains six chapters. The first chapter outlines the Humpty Dumpty Effect and explains what it is. I demonstrate my research that I conducted for the book and explain how all of this fits together. The remaining chapters each look at a particular demonstration of the Humpty Dumpty Effect in the Scriptures and

---

[3] If a school wants to award me with an honorary doctorate for writing this book, I wouldn't say no.

[4] Just as it is with most stories, the book is always better than the movie. Movies and portrayals about the Bible are great, but they cannot take the place of the Text of the Bible.

dive into the history behind it. One may call these "case studies" for the Humpty Dumpty Effect. I do my best to come to some sense of a resolution to how we approach and think about the particular Texts in question. Ultimately, I hope to leave with the reader a desire to study God's Word on a deeper level—sometimes even researching outside of the Text itself in order to understand it better[5]—and to view the Text as primary.

Some Notes about the Book

- This book is written for anyone who wants to read it. I do have a focus on laypeople—those without any formalized education in biblical studies or ministry. I have included extra content to help people learn terms and ideas that are used in the book and to gain a greater understanding of the world of the Bible. Clergy and those in biblical studies will likely be familiar with most of the terms and concepts mentioned, but the content will likely be new. All in all, there is great content for all readers.

- This book combines both academia and my own sense of humor. It is true that I am a geek, but I am a cool Bible geek.

- You are highly encouraged to read the footnotes in the book.[6] References are supplied in the footnote for the reader to check where I sourced information that is not my own. Also, I include a lot of detailed thoughts, humorous quips, and extras in the footnotes. Using footnotes keeps the main text on point rather than looking like the book was written by a squirrel with an espresso addiction.

- Isn't it sad how the older we get, the fewer pictures there are in our books? I include a decent amount of pictures in this book. Pictures help in describing my points, but we all like pictures in our books.

---

[5] Do not misunderstand this statement as contradicting my main point. We view God's Word, the Holy Scriptures, as sacred and inspired literature. But like all literature, it is written in a certain language, in a certain culture, in a different time period than our own. At times, Scripture passages touch on things outside of the Text. Thus, knowledge of these things provides greater clarity and understanding to the Text itself.

[6] This is a footnote. Hello.

א   When referring to the Bible or a passage of it, I often identify it as the Text, with a capital T. This isn't necessary grammatically, but it is my own personal style for this book. It also helps to differentiate it between what is canon and what is not.

א   A glossary is provided in the book to help the reader with some terms that are used in the book. If you don't have a strong background in biblical studies, you may find it helpful to read through it before reading the main chapters. At the very least, learning these words can impress your pastor or friends at church!

CHAPTER 1:
THE HUMPTY DUMPTY EFFECT

"When I use a word, it means just what I choose it to mean---neither more nor less."

—Humpty Dumpty, Through the Looking Glass

My toddler son was watching a nursery rhymes video while I was working on a sermon. This children's video depicted an animated version of "Humpty Dumpty" from the classic nursery rhyme. I turned my gaze away from my commentary and looked at the anthropomorphic[1] egg. As the fictional egg pranced around, I realized something: the nursery rhyme never says that Humpty Dumpty is an egg!

Consider the lyrics for this classic nursery rhyme and notice how there is no overt reference to the character being an egg.

> *Humpty Dumpty sat on a wall,*
> *Humpty Dumpty had a great fall.*
> *All the king's horses and all the king's men*
> *Couldn't put Humpty together again.*

The earliest known publication of this ditty is from Samuel Arnold's *Juvenile Amusements* published in 1797.[2] It was likely around many years prior to that date. The exact origins of this nursery rhyme are murky. Various options are put forward to explain where the phrase "Humpty Dumpty" and the associated poem came from. One theory is that Humpty Dumpty refers to a cannon that was used during the English Civil War. Personally, I find this one to be the most compelling, but certainly I am not an English (or a nursery rhyme) historian. This theory asserts that a cannon that was called Humpty Dumpty sat upon the wall of the fortified city of Colchester. The army on the side of the current king, Charles I, was within the city and used the cannon to keep the Parliamentary forces at bay. Eventually, the Parliamentary forces were able to attack and knock the cannon down, rendering it broken. Thus, as the poem indicates, the king's horses and men were

---

[1] That is, taking the form of a human.

[2] "Humpty Dumpty," The ABC of It: Why Children's Books Matter, accessed November 20, 2024, https://gallery.lib.umn.edu/exhibits/show/abc-of-it--why-children-s-book/pop-culture/humpty-dumpty.

not able to put Humpty Dumpty together again.[3] Another version of the poem from the early 1800s is similar and lends credence to this origin theory. The ending of this poem's version states, "Threescore men and threescore more cannot place Humpty-Dumpty as he was before."[4]

Which one is Humpty Dumpty?

Although the cannon theory is pretty solid (like most cannons…), other theories exist as to the development of the poem or nursery rhyme. One theory contests that Humpty Dumpty was not a poem about a historical event, but it was originally created as a "riddle rhyme." Such riddle rhymes are found in many languages and cultures throughout the years. It may very well be that the Humpty Dumpty rhyme originated as a riddle rhyme with the answer being the egg we now often think of. Variations of the Humpty Dumpty rhyme are found in other languages throughout Europe.[5] To illustrate the riddle rhyme, notice a similar riddle rhyme to that of Humpty Dumpty from the same time period.

---

[3] Phillips, Rob. "Humpty Dumpty the Cannon, Not the Egg…" Fisher Jones Greenwood Solicitors, February 27, 2015. https://www.fjg.co.uk/blog/humpty-dumpty-cannon-not-egg.

[4] Lina Eckenstein, *Comparative Studies in Nursery Rhymes* (London: Duckworth & Co., 1906), 105.

[5] Eckenstein, 105-106. Other funny titles of these are "Hiimpelken-Pumpelken" and "Gigele-Gagele."

As round as an apple, as deep as a cup,
And all the king's horses cannot pull it up.[6]

The answer to this riddle rhyme is a well. While it is not known for certain, the Humpty Dumpty poem may have originally been a riddle rhyme describing an egg.

Riddle rhymes aside, you may be shell-shocked to hear that there are still more theories for the original meaning of "Humpty Dumpty." Going back to the 17th century, a type of alcoholic drink was called a Humpty Dumpty (ale boiled in brandy…which sounds both bad tasting and bad for your health).[7] The Oxford English Dictionary also informs us that during that time period "an ill-shaped, hapless, overweight person" was called a Humpty Dumpty.[8] There may even be a correlation with persons with this type of body feature that has led to the development of Humpty Dumpty being an egg. One interesting theory is that the term Humpty Dumpty came to describe someone with Cushing's Syndrome.[9] Cushing's syndrome often presents with abdominal weight gain and smaller arms and legs. Note the connection between a person with this type of physical abnormality and the anthropomorphic egg—round body, small appendages. Furthermore, some hypothesize that the Humpty Dumpty rhyme is a reference to King Richard III—an English monarch whom history paints as disfigured and

---

[6] Eckenstein, 107.

[7] Eckenstein, 109.

[8] "Humpty Dumpty Was Code For…," History Daily, October 27, 2022, https://historydaily.org/what-humpty-dumpty-really-means/3.

[9] Lakhani OJ and Lakhani JD, "Endocrinology and 'Humpty Dumpty' *"Indian Journal of Endocrinology and Metabolism* 24 (October 19, 2020): 509–11. Dr. Lakhani notes in the article: "One of the characteristic features of Cushing syndrome is the redistribution of body fat. There is excess fat being deposited in the temporal region leading to moon-like face, in the cervical region, leading to what is known as the "buffalo hump" and in the abdominal region leading to an increase waist circumference. On the other hand, there is loss of muscle mass
from the peripheries leading to what is known as "stick-like" arms and legs. Humpty-Dumpty has a redistribution of fat as we would expect from a patient with Cushing syndrome. He has a moon-like face and central obesity combined with 'stick-like' arms and legs."

hunchbacked.[10] Thus, there are a myriad of theories that seek to explore the historical origins of the phrase "Humpty Dumpty" and the poem. We will likely never know with any certainty about its development.

Not all portrayals of Humpty Dumpty are of an egg. How strange!

Perhaps the greatest factor in the popular modern interpretation of Humpty Dumpty as an egg-man came from the author Lewis Carroll. In 1882, Carroll published the book *Through the Looking Glass and What Alice Found There*. One

---

[10] "Humpty Dumpty Was Code For..." It's difficult to arrive at an unbiased, original description of him because of his role as an English Monarch and his many portrayals in literature (including Shakespeare's *Richard III*).

chapter in the book features Alice talking with Humpty Dumpty. Both the text and the illustration provided by John Tenniel portray Humpty Dumpty as an egg-man.[11] While not all depictions of Humpty Dumpty since Arnold's publication in 1797 are of an anthropomorphic egg, the large majority are. Indeed, you would be hard-pressed (or should we say hard-boiled?) to find any interpretation or illustration of the poem where Humpty Dumpty is not an egg-man since Carroll's book.

A creepy toy bank of Humpty Dumpty.

We can see the obscure history of both the poem about Humpty Dumpty and the phrase "Humpty Dumpty." What started out as one thing may have morphed into something else over time. Here is the crux of the matter: this short poem,

---

[11] Lewis Carroll and John Tenniel, *Through the Looking-Glass, and What Alice Found There* (Philadelphia: Henry Altemus, 1897), 114-133.

throughout multiple centuries of hearing and interpretation, has led to it almost exclusively being interpreted as a poem about an egg.

Why is that???

After spending a considerable amount of time mulling over this idea, coupled with my interest in biblical studies, I have identified a phenomenon that I would like to refer to as "the Humpty Dumpty Effect." A specific interpretation or depiction of a text can develop over time so that it becomes universally accepted (or at least widely known) even though the text itself doesn't conclusively lead itself to that interpretation. In other words, Humpty Dumpty was depicted as an egg and people continue to think/view of it as an egg.

In the history of biblical interpretation, certain texts get portrayed or understood in some way and it becomes commonplace to think of them as such. This may be the case even though a specific text never overtly mentions that detail. For an introductory example, consider the narrative from Acts chapter 9 where Saul is traveling to Damascus. When I was in college, one of my professors was referring to the event and mentioned how Saul fell off his donkey. One student raised his hand and remarked, "Sir, the Text never says that Saul was riding on a donkey." Despite knowing his Bible very well, this Christian ministry professor had succumbed to the Humpty Dumpty Effect. For centuries it has commonly been assumed that Saul was riding on a horse or donkey when Jesus spoke to him. Myriad art pieces depict the conversion of Saul with a donkey/horse in the picture even though the Scripture Text says nothing of any mode of transportation.[12]

---

[12] He could have been skipping or riding a scooter for all we know.

Painting on bowl by Francesco Xanto Avelli (1525).
Imagine eating cereal from this bowl!

Just like the Humpty Dumpty poem, various Scripture narratives get portrayed in a certain way, and that interpretation becomes commonplace. In this book, I shall explore with the reader the Humpty Dumpty Effect in regard to biblical interpretation. First, I will share my own research which I have conducted to test the Humpty Dumpty Effect. After this, I will provide a closer look at some of the Scripture passages where the effect is commonly seen. In these chapters, I present the Text, explain how it is commonly interpreted, and the development of the Text's interpretation over time. At various points in the book, I devote space to relevant topics to the particular Text that are being examined. I also supply some fun and insightful "detours" on the way. All throughout the pages of this book, I hope the reader can see why this all matters and what we ought to do about the Humpty Dumpty Effect.

Surveys and Spambots

My initial research into the Humpty Dumpty Effect largely took place informally by noticing how people interpreted some passages of Scripture. I noticed how often little things would stick out in someone's explanation of a passage of Scripture which is not found in the Text. My interest in this peaked. I began to ask people about certain passages which are frequently associated with the Humpty Dumpty Effect. I continued to notice the effect.

When I decided to write about the Humpty Dumpty Effect, I knew it would be best to do a survey so that specific examples could be paired with numbers. I will include most of the technical information about the survey in a footnote.[13] It is important to share some information about the audience for the survey. In general, those who took the survey have above average knowledge of the Bible.[14] The majority of participants attend church frequently, and a very large majority identity themselves as Christians. I wanted to test the effect on those who know their Bible and how it affects their interpretation. I would imagine that the survey results would look significantly different if the general population of the nation (which would include more non-Christians and those with less biblical knowledge) were surveyed. The above-average biblical knowledge expressed in the surveys is important as it demonstrates how people who are well-versed in Scripture fall prey to the Humpty Dumpty Effect. As you can see in the chart, many have a high degree of biblical knowledge with over half having taken Bible classes in college.

---

[13] The majority of surveys were completed online via Google Docs. A small number were completed on paper. There was no difference between the online surveys and the paper surveys.
Survey questions asked for faith affiliation, level of church attendance, self-rating of biblical knowledge, and what type of biblical education people have.
Questions were posed so as not to lead people in answering. This was completed by avoiding multiple choice and asking survey participants to answer directly. As an example, when surveying persons about the narrative from Genesis 3, I asked them to summarize the passage and include any relevant details. I did not include any reference to specific things I was looking for in responses.
[14] Based on a scale of 1-10, the average score from the surveys is 6.95. Only a small number of responses were 4 or below.

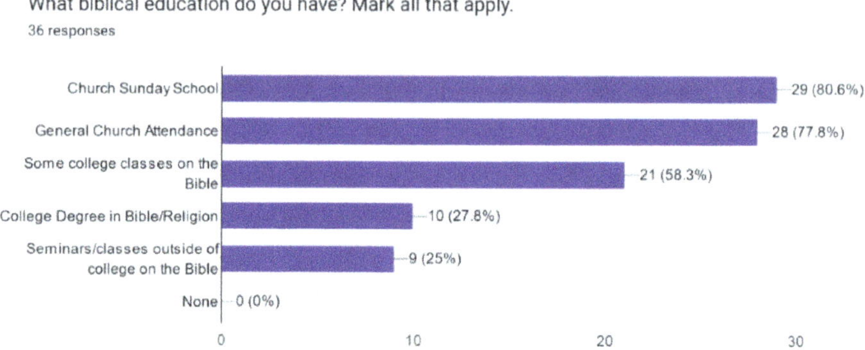

As part of the survey, I asked participants to select from a list of 8 statements which were actually Bible verses. The statements were as follows. Those that are actual Bible verses are shown with their references:

"Cleanliness is next to godliness for a righteous man ought to keep his house in order."

"Children, obey your parents in the Lord, for this is right." (Ephesians 6:1)

"For the love of money is a root of all kinds of evil." (1 Timothy 4:10)

"Remember, brothers and sisters, that when your praises go up, God's blessings come down."

"God won't give you more than you can handle."

"The Lord will help those who help themselves; be not wary of doing right and labor with all your might."

"As a dog returns to its vomit, so fools repeat their folly." (Proverbs 26:11)

"Many who are first will be last, and many who are last will be first." (Matthew 19:30)

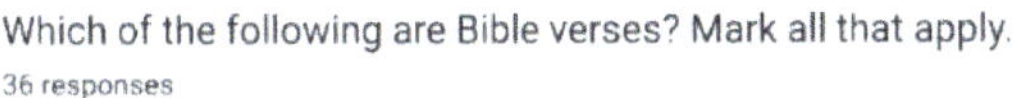

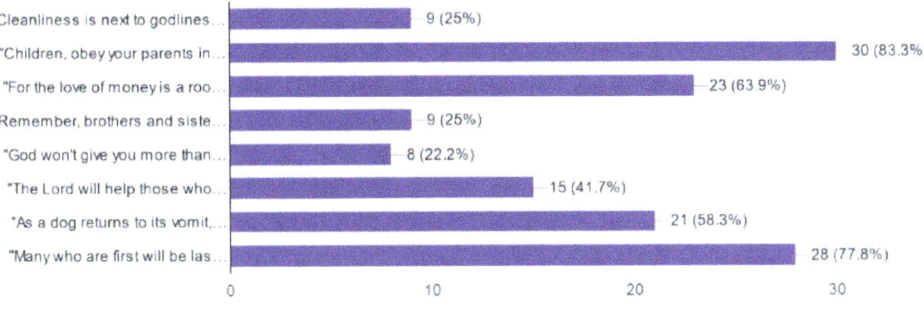

Some of the statements are often quoted and falsely believed to be Scripture. In accordance with the Humpty Dumpty Effect, I surmise that people hear them enough (even mentioned in Christian conversation) that they believe the statements to be from the Bible. As one example, over 40% of survey participants believed that the statement about the Lord helping those who help themselves was from Scripture. Keep in mind that the collective results of the survey show an above average knowledge of the Bible. Yet, many surveys falsely attributed some statements to Scripture, and they did not successfully choose those that were actual Bible verses.

With this being my first time doing research on my own, it was a learning experience. I am grateful for the data that I received. It helped me to see the Humpty Dumpty Effect in a statistical manner. Of course, more data is always better! Yet, as I made the survey public and encouraged people on social media to do the survey, I encountered a problem for which I was not prepared. SPAM BOTS![15] In a short amount of time, I received hundreds and hundreds of completed surveys. At first, I was ecstatic. "Look at all these people filling out my survey. This is awesome!" I thought to myself. Then I realized that these were not humans filling out the forms. "Uh-Oh" as my youngest would say. With all this being shared, I would like to specifically emphasize two points with my readers.

---

[15] These are fully automated computer programs filling out surveys or causing other trouble. They are not robots making Spam. Somehow that seems just as bad.

First, if you ever plan to do any sort of online surveys, take the extra time to prevent spam bots from infiltrating your research. Second, I want to confirm to you that the research shared in this study is of human origin. A great amount of time was spent sifting through individual responses and confirming that an actual person filled out each form. I erred on the side of caution, likely throwing out a few human responses rather than accidentally letting in any spam bot surveys. Thus, the data used in this study is authentic and valid. Now that we have covered the survey and its general results, let us turn to the passages of Scripture where we commonly find the Humpty Dumpty Effect employed.

An adapted story about Humpty Dumpty as an egg.
Created by W. W. Denslow in 1903.

MISUNDERSTOOD AND MISQUOTED

For the love of money is a root of all kinds of evil. Some people, eager for money, have wandered from the faith and pierced themselves with many griefs. (1 Timothy 6:10)

Many misquote Paul's words to Timothy by saying money is the root of all evil (instead of the love of money as a root of all kinds/sorts of evil). The King James Version doesn't render this verse as well as most modern translations. That version says that "the love of money is the root of all evil."

Money by itself is neutral and can be used for good or bad purposes. If money itself were evil, then the Church would not be in the business of collecting offering or holding any currency. The real issue is when someone's desire for money threatens their allegiance to Christ. After all, Jesus said we cannot serve both God and money.

Do not judge, or you too will be judged. For in the same way you judge others, you will be judged, and with the measure you use, it will be measured to you. Why do you look at the speck of sawdust in your brother's eye and pay no attention to the plank in your own eye? (Matthew 7:1-3)

These verses, spoken by Jesus, are often misunderstood or read without the entire context. Jesus' message is misunderstood here when the reader presumes that Jesus is forbidding judging altogether. It is true we cannot fully judge someone's intentions, and we certainly cannot make a judgment about someone's eternity destiny—that judgment belongs to Jesus alone. Yet, in life we make judgments. Jesus says in John 7:24: "Stop judging by mere appearances, but instead judge correctly." The problem isn't judging but *how* we judge.

What Jesus warns against is a critical manner of judging that fails to look at oneself. Jesus offers the illustration of a person who is concerned about a speck of sawdust in another's eye but fails to pay attention to the 2x4 wood plank in their own eye. What is the measure or manner with which we judge others? Hopefully, it's with a little more grace than a former teacher I had who marked my math problem wrong because my answer was "12 kids" instead of "12 students." In her judgment, my answer wasn't specific enough to distinguish between human children and baby goats (true story). Confusion about baby goats aside, we should all try to have grace for one another and not hold others to a higher standard than ourselves.

CHAPTER 2:
THE "APPLE" IN GENESIS 3

> *"Of Man's first disobedience, and the fruit*
> *Of that forbidden tree whose mortal taste*
> *Brought death into the World, and all our woe."*
>
> —John Milton in "Paradise Lost."

The first passage I would like to examine goes all the way back to the beginning. Genesis chapter 3 contains the narrative of Adam and Eve in the Garden of Eden. While in the Garden, the original couple eat the forbidden fruit from the "tree in the middle of the garden," referring to the tree of the knowledge of good and evil (cf. Gen. 2:17). In accordance with the Humpty Dumpty Effect, many believe this specific fruit was an apple. Yet, the Text never specifies what type of fruit it is. Notice what is said in Genesis 3:1-6.

Now the serpent was more crafty than any of the wild animals
the LORD God had made. He said to the woman, "Did God
really say, 'You must not eat from any tree in the garden'?"

The woman said to the serpent, "We may eat **fruit** from the
trees in the garden, but God did say, 'You must not eat **fruit**
from the tree that is in the middle of the garden, and you must
not touch it, or you will die.'"

"You will not certainly die," the serpent said to the woman.
"For God knows that when you eat from it your eyes will be
opened, and you will be like God, knowing good and evil."

When the woman saw that the **fruit** of the tree was good for
food and pleasing to the eye, and also desirable for gaining
wisdom, she took some and ate it. She also gave some to her
husband, who was with her, and he ate it. (bold font added)

Many readers automatically assume that the fruit in question is an apple. The Text
in Genesis is straightforward and never mentions what type of fruit it is. The
Hebrew word for fruit, *peri*, is used in these verses. It simply means "fruit." The
passage contains no indication or allusion to what type of fruit it was beyond it
being "good for food and pleasing to the eye, and also desirable for gaining
wisdom."[1] If the author of Genesis 3 wanted to convey specifically that it was an
apple, then why choose the generic word of "fruit?" The Hebrew word for apple
is *tapûaḥ* (תַּפּוּחַ) and is used a few times in the Old Testament. According to
James Strong, this Hebrew word denotes generally an apple but could also be
applied to other pome fruits such as pears and quinces.[2] It seems clear that if the
author of Genesis 3 wanted to declare it was an apple, then tapûaḥ would have
been used instead of peri.

---

[1] Since it was pleasing to the eye, we can definitely rule out Ugli Fruit!

[2] James Strong, *The New Strong's Exhaustive Concordance of the Bible: With Main
Concordance, Appendix to the Main Concordance, Topical Index to the Bible,
Dictionary of the Hebrew Bible, Dictionary of the Greek Testament* (Nashville: T.
Nelson, 1984), 125.

Though the Text does not infer that the forbidden fruit was an apple, modern-day interpretations and portrayals of this narrative often have Adam and Eve eating an apple. Consider how many times you have seen a picture of Adam and Eve in the Garden of Eden eating an apple. My son's kindergarten teacher was once sharing the story of Adam and Eve with the class, and she stated they sinned by eating the apple. I politely corrected her that no apple is mentioned in the Text. My son's teacher is definitely not alone in making this assumption. Consider the two images below which demonstrate the Humpty Dumpty Effect in regard to the apple.

An AI Engine was asked to create an image of Adam and Eve in the garden. This is the result.

Even AI engines tend to think of the forbidden fruit as an apple.

My survey reflects that a few people hold the assumption that the fruit in Genesis 3 was an apple. When asked to share details from this narrative, over 8% voluntarily listed that Adam and Eve ate an apple.[3] I believe a poll of the general population would demonstrate a much higher belief that the fruit in question is an apple. I discovered informal support for this belief when my family and I visited the Ark Encounter in Williamstown, Kentucky. Inside this true-to-scale replica of Noah's ark was a depiction of Adam and Eve in the garden with what appeared to be a bushel of grapes—this was the forbidden fruit. Many visitors shared their surprise that it was not an apple. Whenever we think about or visualize the forbidden fruit, the apple keeps coming to mind. How did this come to be?

Before proceeding further into this discussion, I want to share my approach to the Old Testament Texts that will be examined. Jewish sources will be utilized when they are helpful to see the development and interpretation of any of the selected biblical Texts. You may wonder why I would research specifically Jewish approaches when this paper is written from a Christian perspective. First and foremost, the Old Testament Texts were around for centuries prior to the arrival of Christ. Texts would have known and interpreted for an extended period of time before the advent of Christianity. Understanding how early Jewish sources interpreted our Texts can help us to arrive at a better understanding of its interpretive history.

Second, Jewish sources are utilized because both Jews and Christians share a common sacred literature—a "common bible"[4] if you will. The 39 books of the Old Testament are viewed by Jews as sacred and authoritative. Referred to as the Tanakh, these books are the foundational text for the Jewish faith. You will often

---

[3] I did not want to steer answers as a way to uphold my theory, so I asked people to share what they knew about the passage. My guess is that if the question was asked if there was an apple or not in the passage, the results would be higher. Specifically, I phrased the survey in this way: Without using a Bible or Bible app, please summarize the narrative from Genesis chapter 3 with Adam and Eve in the Garden of Eden. Share any knowledge or details that you have of the narrative from the time they were created and placed in the garden until they were kicked out.

[4] Terminology used by Emmanouela Grypeou and Helen Spurring. I shall reference them again.

see it referred to as the Hebrew Bible.[5] Although there are minor differences between the Christian Old Testament and the Tanakh, the two contain, in essence, the same content and the same books. Thus, we can find early interpretations from this literature from two religious groups giving us additional insight.

Third, interpretations of the Old Testament/Tanakh were developed together by Jews and Christians, especially during the period of Late Antiquity.[6] This time period "marks the formation and development of Christianity and rabbinic Judaism as religious systems."[7] Although distinct religious groups, the two groups interacted socially and would influence one another (archaeological evidence supports this notion).[8] For our sake, this would have been true in regard to interpretation of the Old Testament/Hebrew Bible. Studies exist that analyze the use of Jewish sources by early Christian authors.

Rambling aside, this is what I want the reader to note: textual interpretation did not (nor does it ever) occur in a vacuum.[9] For Christians and Jews in this period, there were likely exegetical encounters that occurred which would have affected interpretation going forward.[10] As we look at the Genesis Text, we will see how religious tradition influences textual interpretation.

---

[5] The term "Bible" is used in different ways. While Christians refer to our sacred text as the Holy Bible, the term is also used to describe any sacred or authoritative text for a religious group, i.e. Jewish Bible. It may also be used, perhaps sacrilegiously, as a supreme or preeminent text regardless of the topic. Although I don't like the name, *The Grilling Bible* supplies some wonderful recipes.

[6] Approximately 250-750 AD

[7] Emmanouela Grypeou and Helen Spurling, *The Book of Genesis in Late Antiquity: Encounters between Jewish and Christian Exegesis* (Leiden: Brill, 2013), 2.

[8] Grypeou and Spurling, 5.

[9] To speak of something in a vacuum means to understand something without any other influences. This is often done in science. The well-known speed of light (3×10^8 m/s) assumes it is in a vacuum (thanks, Emily, for teaching me this). The actual speed becomes slower depending on what medium it travels through or if it needs to pick up milk on the way home.

[10] Grypeou and Spurling, 26. This book examines the possible opportunities Jewish and Christian sources interacted in regard to interpretation in the book of Genesis. The

Returning to Genesis 3, let us consider the thoughts and interpretations put forth by Jewish rabbis and early Christian authors on the Text. Jewish rabbis provide a variety of interpretations regarding the tree and the fruit from which Eve and Adam ate. The following rabbinical interpretations come from 400 AD or earlier.[11] Multiple rabbis argue that the tree in question is actually wheat even though the Text mentions a tree. In particular, Rabbi Ze'eira argues that "it [the wheat in Eden] rose to a great height, like the cedars of Lebanon."[12] Perhaps the wheat was able to grow so tall because it was gluten-free (or maybe gluten came to be part of the wheat after the fall…). Rabbi Yehuda bar Ilai wrote that the fruit Adam and Eve ate were grapes. He quotes from Deuteronomy 32:32 in his defense. The verse reads: "Their grapes are filled with poison, and their clusters with bitterness." Thus, the couple brought bitterness into the world by eating these grapes.[13] Rabbi Abba of Akko believed the fruit was a citron. This rabbi arrives at this conclusion due to the Text saying that the tree is good for eating—implying that the tree itself (not the fruit) is delicious.[14] Bark…Yum! Several other rabbis argue that the infamous fruit was a fig. Rabbi Yosei makes his argument from the context of Genesis 3, recalling how Adam and Eve made clothes out of fig leaves. Two other rabbis hypothesize specific fig genera. Rabbi Avin argues the fruit was "the *berat sheva* species, as it brought seven [*sheva*] days of mourning to the world."[15] And Rabbi Yehoshua believes the fruit "was the *berat elita* species, as it brought weeping [*elita*] to the world."[16] Lastly, Rabbi Azarya and Rabbi Yehuda bar Simon theorize

---

authors define an encounter as "an exegetical tradition that appears to show awareness of, or a response to, a tradition from the writings of the other religious group."

[11] Jason Rappoport, ed., "Bereshit Rabbah," trans. Joshua Schreier, Sefaria, accessed November 12, 2023, https://www.sefaria.org/Bereshit_Rabbah. This Jewish writing is described as" a talmudic-era midrash on the book of Genesis. It interprets most of Genesis (with the exception of genealogies and such) with verse-by-verse and often word-by-word commentary."

[12] Bereshit Rabbah 15:7

[13] Bereshit Rabbah 15:7

[14] Bereshit Rabbah 15:7

[15] Bereshit Rabbah 15:7

[16] Bereshit Rabbah 15:7

that God chooses not to reveal the specific type of fruit to Adam's descendants lest it leads to future problems.[17]

After researching what early rabbis thought about the fruit from the tree of knowledge, I looked into what the early Church Fathers had to say about it. This is what I found:

That's right—Nothing! After many hours of research and looking into sources of the early Church Fathers, I was unable to find any specific reflection or discussion concerning what type of fruit Adam and Eve ate. Within its first few centuries of existence, Christianity had a lot of doctrinal duty to accomplish. The early Church Fathers spent much time and energy properly explaining and defending their faith in a world that encompassed many different beliefs. When they turned their attention to Genesis 3, we note their concern for application of the Text and how the Old Testament (which would not have been called the Old Testament originally) connected to faith in Jesus Christ. What I discovered is that these early Church theologians were more interested in *typology* than the *type* of fruit mentioned in Genesis 3.

Typology has nothing to do with your computer's keyboard. Rather, typology involves studying the Bible to identify items in the Old Testament that foreshadow something in the New Testament. These "types" can be persons, events, or institutions that look forward to fulfillment in Jesus Christ and the New Covenant.[18] These types exist because of the connection between the Old and New Testaments, with God paving the way for what was to come. The theologians of the early years of the Church focused on these typological connections between the Old and New Testaments. For our case, they were drawn to the types found in Genesis chapter 3.

The relatively short passage of Scripture is home to several types that look forward to the New Covenant. The most common one is that of Adam and Christ. Even

---

[17] Bereshit Rabbah 15:7

[18] William Coker, "Type, Typology," essay, in Beacon Dictionary of Theology, ed. J. Kenneth Grider, Willard H. Taylor, and Richard S Taylor (Kansas City, Mo: Beacon Hill Press of Kansas City, 1983), 532–33.

the Apostle Paul talks about this typology (see 1 Cor. 15:21-22 and Romans 5:12-19). Other common types found here are Eve foreshadowing Mary and the tree of the knowledge of good and evil foreshadowing the cross. Let us observe how some of the early Church Fathers would have looked at this last type. Hence, we begin our first voyage into **LATIN**[19].

IT'S ALL LATIN TO ME!!!

Look at these two verses in Latin. Notice the same word used in the verses from Old and New Testaments.

Genesis 3:6: Vidit igitur mulier quod bonum esset lignum ad vescendum, et pulchrum oculis, aspectuque delectabile: et tulit de fructu illius, et comedit: deditque viro suo, qui comedit.

Galatians 3:13: Christus nos redemit de maledicto legis, factus pro nobis maledictum: quia scriptum est: Maledictus omnis qui pendet in ligno[20].

The Latin word "lignum" means tree or wood. Those early Church Fathers who read and wrote in Latin would have recognized the connection between the two testaments and saw the typology there. The Greek Bishop Irenaeus articulates this important typology early in the history of the Christian Church. According to biblical scholar Stephen Presley, "Irenaeus discusses the passion of Christ in correspondence with the disobedience of Adam. Through his passion, Christ undoes the effects of the disobedience that transpired in the beginning at the 'tree' (ligno, Gen 3:6)…The catchword ligno combines with the asymmetrical relationship of Adam and Christ's actions toward God."[21] Irenaeus and many other

---

[19] I have been able to learn Koine Greek and Hebrew, but I have never formally studied Latin. Yet, it's not difficult to pick up on some of its usage especially since it uses the same alphabet as English. Sadly, Pig Latin has always been a struggle for me. Que triste 😦

[20] Red font added by me. Different noun endings account for the slight variation at the end of the word.

[21] Stephen O. Presley, *The Intertextual Reception of Genesis 1-3 in Irenaeus of Lyons* (Leiden: Brill, 2015), 208.

theologians of the early years of the Church focused on the typology rather than botany.

Who started talking about the forbidden fruit first? The earliest reference to any description of the tree and its fruit is found in the book of 1 Enoch. The book of 1 Enoch is not considered Scripture by either Jews or Christians. It is part of what is commonly referred to as the Pseudepigrapha[22] (don't feel bad if you have trouble reading or pronouncing that word!). In 1 Enoch, there is a scene where Enoch (from Genesis) sees the tree of wisdom and describes it: "That tree is in height like the fir, and its leaves are like (those of) the Carob tree: and its fruit is like the clusters of the vine, very beautiful: and the fragrance of the tree penetrates afar."[23] Certainly sounds more like grapes than an apple! So again, how in the world did we end up with an apple as our forbidden fruit?

There are two prominent theories that explain how the apple became our chosen forbidden fruit. Both of these involve an etymological mistake—one with Latin (again), and one with French. The first theory that bears fruit[24] regards a similarity between two Latin words: *malum* and *malus*.[25] In Genesis 3:5, the serpent tells Eve that eating the fruit will cause her to be like God, knowing good and evil (malum*).* Malum is pretty similar to the Latin word for apple, malus. Likely due to the mix-up of these two words, the apple became commonly seen as the forbidden fruit.

The second theory holds that the apple became commonly understood as the forbidden fruit starting in 12th century France. According to Professor Azzan Yadin-Israel the development of the Old French word for fruit, *pom*, is to blame. At that time, pom simply meant "fruit" —any fruit at all. Over time, the word pom came to describe an apple instead of a generic term for any fruit.[26] Thus,

---

[22] See full description in my glossary. In short, they are writings penned as if a hero of the faith wrote them. They are not in the canon of Scripture.

[23] 1 Enoch 1:34. Robert Henry Charles, ed., *The Apocrypha and Pseudepigrapha of the Old Testament. 1, Apocrypha* (Oxford: Clarendon Press, 1983).

[24] All puns are intended.

[25] Ziony Zevit, *What Really Happened in the Garden of Eden?* (New Haven: Yale University Press, 2013), 170.

[26] "How the Forbidden Fruit Became an Apple," Rutgers University, February 26, 2023, https://www.rutgers.edu/news/how-forbidden-fruit-became-apple.

readers in French would come to read and understand our passage in question as Adam and Eve eating an apple. Historical linguistics certainly can and do affect our understanding of past things!

As you can see from the examination of the Text, there is no evidence to support the idea that the forbidden fruit was an apple. The previously mentioned theories and persistent depictions of the apple as the forbidden fruit have led to many people today naturally assuming that the apple is the culprit for our spiritual downfall. To the delight of orchards everywhere, the apple is not the enemy! We will likely not know what type of fruit grew on that tree this side of eternity, but that is probably for the best…We don't want to eat it again. We are not done with this passage though. We find another instance of the Humpty Dumpty Effect in Genesis chapter 3.

Note the obvious allusion to the forbidden fruit.

Imagine attending a worship service at a new church. You settle into your seat (toward the back, obviously—visitors never sit in the front two-thirds of the church) only to be completely surprised at the music that begins to play. Instead of traditional hymns and choruses you hear music commonly played in bars and nightclubs—albeit with the lyrics slightly altered to give a Christian spin. Directly before prayer you hear Bon Jovi's "Living on a Prayer." When the offering is being taken, you hear the party song by Joan Jett with an interesting twist: "I love Jesus Christ; put another dollar in the offering plate, baby!" The pastor preaches on faith and invites the praise team to sing their version of Journey's "Don't Stop Believing." The service ends with Holy Communion, but not without an adapted version of Neil Diamond's "Red, Red Wine" playing in the background.

Continuing the scene, imagine you confront the pastor of this "church" after the service is complete. With a mixture of great offense and confusion, you inquire why the church is using these secular songs as part of their musical worship. The pastor provides this theological explanation: John and Charles Wesley adapted the lyrics from the tavern songs of their day to evangelize to the common man, and we are doing the same.

Is that true? Did John and Charles Wesley, the founders of Methodism, adapt drinking songs and convert them into the hymns they wrote?

No.

It has been a fairly common myth for decades that these men adapted the tunes sung in taverns into hymns. Upon further investigation, this is a misapplication caused by historical linguistics. The culprit is a difference in how words were used then and now. A music term known as "bar form" or "bar tune" indicates that a song uses repeated lines. Many of the Wesley hymns incorporate this bar form. Instead of people referring to these worship songs as being written in bar form, they probably called them bar songs. As we can see, John and Charles did not frequent the local pubs looking for their next musical inspiration.[27]

To call something a "bar song" today has a much different connotation than it would have at that time. The development of language over time results in some funny interpretations and application, and this is an example that hits close to "church."

Perhaps historians in the future will develop interesting interpretations for our current society based on how language changes over time. I can only wonder if Taylor Swift will be viewed as a 21st century female version of Genghis Khan with often how she *slayed* at her concerts.

---

[27] "No Conversion for Tavern Tunes," The Washington Times, August 21, 2002, https://www.washingtontimes.com/news/2002/aug/21/20020821-041030-4581r/.

CHAPTER 3:
THE SERPENT AS SATAN IN GENESIS 3

"You are the devil, and the devil is bad!"

—The W's

Then the Lord God said to the woman,
"What is this you have done?"
The woman said, "The serpent deceived me, and I ate."
So the Lord God said to the serpent,
"Because you have done this,
"Cursed are you above all livestock
and all wild animals!
You will crawl on your belly
and you will eat dust
all the days of your life.
And I will put enmity
between you and the woman,
and between your offspring and hers;
he will crush your head,
and you will strike his heel."

(Genesis 3:13-15)

For our second instance of the Humpty Dumpty Effect, we return to the same scene—Adam and Eve in the Garden of Eden. As you read and imagine in your mind how this passage plays out, you may have visualized the snake/serpent as Satan taking on a devious form. Yet, you may be surprised to hear that the Text never identifies the serpent as Satan. This is a very common interpretation of the Text. In my survey, I asked participants to summarize the narrative of Adam and

Eve from the Garden of Eden. Without asking them specifically about the temptation, the snake or the fruit, 24% of participants voluntarily include Satan/the devil as tempting Eve in their responses.[1] I have also noticed this repeatedly noted in Sunday School lessons, sermons, and other general discussion of this Text. In fact, I literally just asked my two oldest sons about this passage, and they both said the serpent was the devil.[2] So, where did this interpretation come from and why is it so popular?

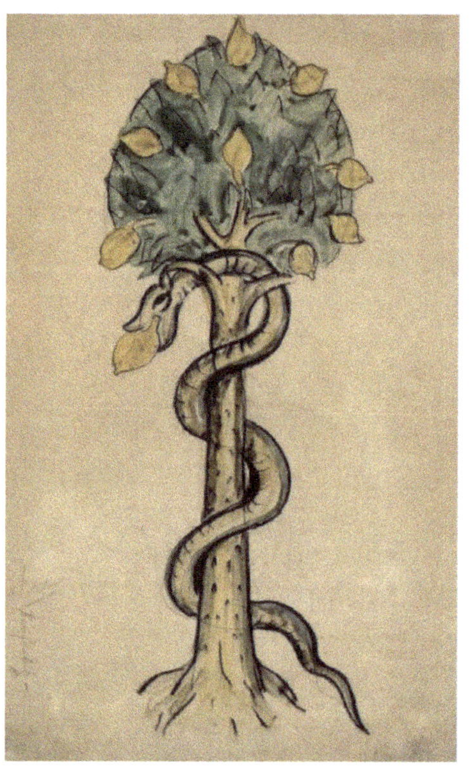

"The Garden of Eden Serpent" by Russian artist El Lissitzky.

---

[1] My survey questions were intentionally open-ended so as not to steer questions into a desired result. My children are afraid of the dark because they know of it and are aware of it. They have never had any bedtime phobias about the Chupacabra because we have never talked about it. I imagine if I specifically asked about who/what tempted Eve the results would be significantly higher.

[2] Thankfully not the Chupacabra.

In order to know where this popular interpretation comes from, we need to examine the history and understanding of this foundational biblical text. We will first look closely at the Text in question and then explore its understanding/interpretation throughout the ages, including both Jewish and Christian perspectives.

Our passage from Genesis 3 contains four main characters: God, Adam, Eve, and the serpent. Satan (or any other names by which he goes) is never mentioned. Many interpretations of the Text insert Satan as the serpent. The Hebrew word for serpent in this passage is *nahash,* and it just means serpent. The word is used many other times throughout the Old Testament, and in those other cases, it is just talking about a serpent.

Furthermore, the person (or entity) of Satan does not appear in Genesis 3. The Hebrew word for Satan is שָׂטָן, but we can use its transliteration, *satan.* I know, it's pretty easy to remember! Satan is not found at all in the passage. The general use of the term throughout the Old Testament contrasts with its use in the New Testament. While Satan (or the devil) is the great enemy of God and the Church, in the Old Testament the word satan has not come to fully mean that yet. Many interpret this word usage in the book of Job as referring to God's great enemy, and the context fits.[3] However, the Hebrew term simply refers to someone who is an adversary or an accuser. We see accounts in the Old Testament where the term refers to God's great enemy (as in Job) and other times where it simply means a person who opposes another. For instance, 1 King 5:4 in the KJV says: "But now the LORD my God hath given me rest on every side, so that there is neither *adversary* nor evil occurrent."[4] King Solomon is stating that the Lord has given him and the nation rest so there are no literal enemies. It does not invoke a sense of Satan—God's great enemy. All in all, the term satan is used less than 30 times in

---

[3] This is not to imply that this it is universally accepted that Satan in Job is the devil. However, the Text can easily be interpreted and read as such.

[4] Emphasis added by me.

the Old Testament, with the majority of those referring to God's enemy in the book of Job.[5]

Following the order of the Canon of Scripture, the first use of satan is found in Numbers 22:22. In this verse, the angel of the Lord stands as an adversary/satan to stop the prophet Balaam from going on his current path. Clearly, the angel is doing the work of the Lord and is not God's enemy. I also highlight this first use of the word to show the large gap (in time and literature) between Genesis 3 and Numbers 22 (this latter passage has no allusion to God's great enemy). So, how in the garden did we end up understanding the serpent as Satan/the devil?

I shall now explain how the serpent in the Genesis 3 came to be understood as Satan. Please note that I am not providing a <u>thorough</u> study about the devil and his development throughout Scripture and time. There are many books that address this detailed topic. Later in this section I will briefly touch upon the doctrine of Satan for Christian and Jewish faiths. For now, I want to look at snakes in the Bible.

SNAKES—GOOD, BAD, OR UGLY?

The modern opinion on snakes is fairly negative; most people don't like snakes. They are viewed as creepy, icky, and scary. Most people cringe at the thought of having a pet snake or encountering a snake in the wild. Yet, earlier cultures and societies did not necessarily share our general disdain for these creatures. Ophidian[6] images have been found in many ancient cultures, some of these are still part of our collective knowledge and imagery today, typically behind the scenes. According to Old Testament professor Dr. Elaine Phillips, the serpent has carried both positive and negative connotations. Serpents in the ancient Near East were regarded as metaphors for a variety of things, ranging from life and fertility to chaos and death.[7] Likewise, James Charlesworth notes that out of the 46 ancient

---

[5] The other appearances are: 1 Chronicles 21:1; Psalm 109:6; Zecheriah 3:1, 2, Num. 22:22, 32; 1 Samuel 29:4; 1 Kings 5:4, 11:14, 23, 25.

[6] Term referring to snakes or being snake-like.

[7] Elaine A Phillips, "Serpent Intertexts: Tantalizing Twists in the Tales," *Bulletin for Biblical Research* 10, no. 2 (2000): 233–45, 238.

serpent images he identified, 28 are positive. He writes, "the serpent is probably the most pervasive symbol in art, sculpture, and literature among the early Jews. Ophidian images and concepts mostly carry a positive connotation."[8]

The staff of Aesculapius is an ancient Greek symbol representing healing and medicine. It is commonly used today in various forms.

---

[8] James Charlesworth, "Serpent," in *T & T Clark Encyclopedia of Second Temple Judaism*, ed. Daniel M. Gurtner (London: T & T Clark, 2020).

Even if this is true of the early Jews and ancient cultures, for Christians (from the beginning to today) it is hard to see the serpent as positive. Genesis 3 never specifically states the serpent is bad-the serpent is called '*arum*, or crafty. While crafty is not necessarily bad, the serpent's action proves that he is up to no good. The truth is that the serpent in Genesis 3 was the first "bad guy" of the Bible. He questioned the word of the Lord, tempted Eve, and ultimately was the initial adversary/satan for God and His rule.

While there are positive and neutral serpent references in Scripture, there are prominent negative ones which remind us of the serpent in Genesis 3. These references help to bolster the common interpretation of the serpent in Genesis 3 as the devil. One particular Christian author, Brian Everrett, argues that a serpent motif runs throughout all of the Scriptures. After reviewing the events of Genesis 3 and looking at how the serpent shows up in bad ways throughout Scripture, he writes, "In sum, the serpent is one who opposes God. It does this by questioning, lying about, and contradicting God's word, tempting and deceiving the Lord's people, and exercising authority over humanity."[9] In Verrett's view, any of these actions throughout Scripture are an allusion back to the serpent as God's enemy in Genesis 3.

Let's consider a few Old Testament verses that portray the serpent in a negative light.

In the book of 1 Kings, there is a scene where a son of David attempts to set himself up as king over Israel. 1 Kings 1:9-10 reads:

> *Adonijah then sacrificed sheep, cattle and fattened calves at the Stone of Zoheleth near En Rogel. He invited all his brothers, the king's sons, and all the royal officials of Judah, but he did not invite Nathan the prophet or Benaiah or the special guard or his brother Solomon.*

---

[9] Brian A. Verrett, *The Serpent in Samuel: A Messianic Motif* (Eugene, OR: Resource Publications, 2020), 17.

There are two specific connections with the serpent in this Text. First, Adonijah goes to sacrifice animals at the Stone of Zoheleth. Zoheleth most likely means "serpent."[10] Thus, the place where Adonijah tries to improperly offer sacrifices and establish himself as king is at the serpent-stone.[11] As the narrative progresses, we continue to see Adonijah in a negative light, thus creating a connection between the serpent-stone and evil behavior. In the second instance, we see Adonijah acting "crafty" just like the serpent from Genesis 3. He makes a request to the newly pronounced King Solomon through King David's widow, Bathsheba, that he be given Abishag as his wife. At the beginning of 1 Kings, Abishag is brought in as David's "romantic caregiver." Thus, Adonijah's request could be understood as a ploy to regain the throne from Solomon. Crafty indeed…just like the serpent!

We also find two relevant ophidian references in the Prophet Isaiah.

> *In that day, the Lord will punish with his sword—*
> *his fierce, great and powerful sword—*
> *Leviathan the gliding serpent,*
> *Leviathan the coiling serpent;*
> *he will slay the monster of the sea*
> (Isaiah 27:1)

This particular creature is a Leviathan—a serpent of the sea; it is clearly being described as an enemy of God. God will punish this serpent with his sword. This verse is found in a portion of Isaiah that is looking forward to a time when the Lord will deliver His people and bring them into a state of peace. The prophet even speaks about future resurrection for the Lord's people (cf. Isaiah 26:19). It is not difficult to see how many can interpret this serpent as representing the devil—an enemy of the Lord to be punished at the time of resurrection.

---

[10] Verrett, 23.

[11] Sounds like a great wedding venue.

<blockquote>
The wolf and the lamb will feed together,
and the lion will eat straw like the ox,
and dust will be the serpent's food.
They will neither harm nor destroy
on all my holy mountain,"
says the Lord.
(Isaiah 65:25)
</blockquote>

In this passage, the prophet Isaiah paints a picture of the new heavens and the new earth for those who belong to the Lord. It is a time of hope becoming reality. The prophet speaks of long life, blessings, justice, and even a reversal of the course of nature's animals…with the exception of the serpent. The wolf and the lion are now docile and get along with others, even sharing breakfast with the other creatures. Yet, the serpent is still painted as cursed having dust as its food. This hearkens back to the curse the Lord gave the serpent in Genesis 3: "You will crawl on your belly and you will eat dust all the days of your life." This reference of the serpent in Isaiah 65:25 is a definite allusion to the curse from Genesis 3.

The last Old Testament Text to consider is Jeremiah 51:34. Here, the prophet Jeremiah speaks about the devastation that King Nebuchadnezzar and the Babylonian empire has brought upon the Lord's people.

<blockquote>
Nebuchadnezzar king of Babylon has devoured us,
he has thrown us into confusion,
he has made us an empty jar.
Like a serpent he has swallowed us
and filled his stomach with our delicacies,
and then has spewed us out.
</blockquote>

Notice how the Text describes Nebuchadnezzar and his terrible actions: "like a serpent." King Nebuchadnezzar can obviously be viewed as a great enemy of the Lord and His people. The serpent simile continues to show that the serpent is viewed negatively and as an enemy of the Lord. The connection makes sense…great enemy of God, serpent, thus the devil.

The tendency to view the serpent in Genesis 3 as the devil becomes strongest after we look at particular Texts in the New Testament that mention the devil/Satan or serpents. Part of this has to do with the development of theology regarding Satan specifically in Christian thought. I will briefly address later the divergent views of Satan in Jewish and Christian thought. For now, let us look at a few key texts which solidify interpreting the serpent as the devil.

Multiple times in the Gospels enemies of the Lord are referred to as offspring of serpents (or seed of serpents). Bold font is added by me to show relevant words.

> *But when he saw many of the Pharisees and Sadducees*
> *coming to where he was baptizing, he said to them:*
> *"You **brood** of vipers! Who warned you*
> *to flee from the coming wrath?*
> (Matthew 3:7)
> *You **brood** of vipers, how can you*
> *who are evil say anything good?*
> *For the mouth speaks what the heart is full of.*
> (Matthew 12:34)
> *"You **snakes**! You **brood** of vipers!*
> *How will you escape being condemned to hell?*
> (Matthew 23:33)* [12]

The Greek word that the NIV translates as "brood" is γέννημα or gennéma. It means offspring or fruit. Hence, these verses depict God's enemies as being called children of vipers. These verses remind us of the prophetic word from the Genesis 3 Text which proclaims that there will be enmity between the woman's offspring and the offspring of the serpent.

---

[12] Pastors and church leaders should not call people in the church a brood of vipers, no matter how frustrated they are with them. Just don't.

Another noteworthy Text is found in John 8:44. In this biblical scene, a group of Jews is arguing with Jesus and is threatening to kill him. The tension mounts and they appear as Jesus' enemies, not following the will of God the Father. Jesus then says:

> *You belong to your father, the devil, and you want to carry out your father's desires. He was a murderer from the beginning, not holding to the truth, for there is no truth in him. When he lies, he speaks his native language, for he is a liar and the father of lies.*

There are three things to note about this verse. First, Jesus calls these Jews children/offspring of the devil. This is similar to the other times in the Gospels when Jesus calls His enemies offspring of serpents. Second, Jesus remarks that the devil was a liar from the beginning. The assumed reading of the Text is that the beginning He is talking about is the start of the devil's existence. Yet, it can also be understood as a vague reference to Genesis. Lastly, Jesus' description of the devil fits well with a description of the serpent in Genesis 3—the serpent who was dishonest with Eve and tempted her to sin against the Lord.

The Apostle Paul has written an intriguing verse for this discussion. In the conclusion of his letter to the church in Rome, he writes in Romans 16:20:

> *The God of peace will soon crush Satan under your feet.*

This verse is a strong allusion to the prophetic words of the Lord found in Genesis 3:15 in which the Lord says the offspring of the woman will crush the head of the serpent. Both the Hebrew word in Genesis 3:15 and the Greek word in this verse carry the connotation of crushing, shattering, and bringing victory over an enemy.[13] It is fairly easy to read this verse and mentally think of Jesus putting His

---

[13] The Hebrew word translated as "crush" is שׁוּף/shuph. The Greek word translated as "crush" is συντρίβω/suntribó. Both are translated into English as crush, bruise, or break.

foot on the head of a serpent. Thus, we find a strengthening connection between the serpent in Genesis 3 and the devil.

When we get to the book of Revelation, there is little doubt left as to the connection between the devil and the serpent in Genesis 3. In John's vision in Revelation 12:9, we read:

> *The great dragon was hurled down—that ancient serpent*
> *called the devil, or Satan, who leads the whole world*
> *astray. He was hurled to the earth, and his angels with him.*

John makes it clear that this dragon, or ancient serpent, is the devil (or Satan). In fact, the entire chapter of Revelation 12 uses the titles dragon, serpent, and the devil interchangeably. What other ancient serpent would John be speaking of except the one from Genesis 3 (and perhaps in subtle ways in other Scripture passages)? Furthermore, John solidifies this by again making the same reference in Revelation 20:2:

> *He [an angel of the Lord] seized the dragon,*
> *that ancient serpent, who is the devil, or Satan,*
> *and bound him for a thousand years.*

By this point in history with John's Revelation, the serpent in Genesis 3 has essentially become synonymous with God's great enemy, Satan.

WHO IS SATAN/THE DEVIL?

The person or entity of Satan is not entirely clear in the Old Testament. There is no direct explanation or suggestion in the Old Testament about who he is, his origins, his powers, abilities, etc. It is also helpful to note that there are significant differences between the Jewish and Christian understandings of Satan. In modern Judaism, and even in most forms of Judaism throughout the centuries, the entity of Satan has not held a prominent role in its theology. This is especially true when it is compared with Christianity. In modern Judaism, a succinct understanding of

Satan views him as a heavenly prosecutor[14] (like Satan's role in Job), a personified entity of temptation or an evil inclination to do wicked things.[15] In the mystical branches of Judaism, Kabbalah and Hasidism, there is a significant development of Satan. It is written about Kabbalah's viewpoint regarding Satan: "Satan is known in Kabbalah as Sama'el (rendered in some sources as the Great Demon), and the demonic realm generally as the Sitra Achra—literally 'the other side.' The consort of Sama'el (who is mentioned in pre-kabbalistic Jewish literature as well) is Lilith, a mythic figure in Jewish tradition more commonly known as the rebellious first wife of Adam."[16] As you can see, such a belief goes far beyond the revelation of the Old Testament and is not part of traditional Judaism. In short, modern mainstream Judaism views Satan as either a heavenly being which is under God's authority or that he isn't tangibly real but a metaphor to do wrong (sort of like the humorous cartoon portrayal of a character choosing between right and wrong represented by a good or evil angel on either shoulder. In this case, Satan would be the naughty shoulder angel).

In Christianity, Satan is understood differently. He is a personal, rational being; he is not simply a metaphor. There is a scene in the Gospels where the devil tempts Jesus to give up His calling from the Father and serve him (Matthew 4). The New Testament speaks often of Satan's actions and influence, assuring us that he is on the prowl against the Lord's people (1 Peter 5:8 describes him as a roaring lion looking for someone to devour). Satan is God's chief enemy who seeks to destroy the Church and all that is good.[17] The wonderful news is that the New Testament promises us God's victory over Satan. Though the enemy's power is great, the Church is on the winning side!

---

[14] My Jewish Learning, "Do Jews Believe in Satan?," My Jewish Learning, 2022, https://www.myjewishlearning.com/article/satan-the-adversary/.

[15] "Jewish Concepts: Satan," Jewish Virtual Library, 2024, https://www.jewishvirtuallibrary.org/satan.

[16] My Jewish Learning, "Do Jews Believe in Satan?"

[17] https://www.logos.com/grow/satan-in-the-bible/. This is a nice, relatively short article that provides some insights on Satan and what Scripture says about him. I would encourage the reader to check this out as well as other theological resources to learn more.

It would be easy to get lost in a lengthy study about Satan and everything that we know with certainty about him: his origin, his appearance, his domain, his level of influence over believers and non-believers. Such writing would be far beyond the scope of my book! Perhaps you wonder why we don't know more about Satan at the beginning of the Bible (the book of Genesis). With the connection between the serpent in Genesis 3 and Satan, why didn't the author of Genesis come forward and share all the details about this super-duper bad guy?

Imagine that the Lord comes to Adam and Eve in the Garden of Eden and presents two books. The first book is a large book with a picture of a serpent on it; the second is a much larger book that stands almost two cubits high. The Lord says, "This first book is for the two of you so that you can understand your enemy. His name is Satan, and he will likely come to you as a talking serpent. I want you to be prepared for his craftiness."

Adam asks, "What is this second book, Lord?"

The Lord replies, "That very large book is for you, Adam. It is a book on how to understand your wife. I have a second volume for you when you are finished with that one."

As helpful as it would have been to receive a thorough, direct revelation via written instruction (or any form of communication), the Lord has chosen not to operate this way. We find that God has chosen to reveal Himself through progressive revelation. Allison Gregg defines it this way: "God's communication of himself is characterized by development, not it terms of evolutionary advancement or the correction of earlier revelation by later revelation, but it terms of fuller disclosure in successive stages, each building on former ones."[18] We don't have the whole picture of God, His character, and His plan for salvation from the beginning. God reveals it over time. We now have the full picture of God's revelation in Jesus Christ (cf. Hebrews 1:1-3) and in a similar way to God's revelation of Himself, the understanding and disclosure of God's great enemy, the devil, over time. Thus,

---

[18] Gregg R. Allison, *The Baker Compact Dictionary of Theological Terms, EBSCOhost* (Grand Rapids, MI: Baker Books, 2016).

in the New Testament there is much more to be said about the devil than in the Old Testament.

Returning to our Text in Genesis 3, we now see that there is a clear connection demonstrated throughout Scripture between the serpent in the passage and Satan himself. Yet, what exactly is that connection? Was the serpent Satan himself? Was the serpent an ally of Satan? Was the critter coerced by Satan to do his bidding? Or was the serpent a representative or intermediary of the prince of this world? Also worth examining is the nature of the serpent in Genesis 3. As we will see, Jewish rabbis and the early Church Fathers had thoughts on the serpent/Satan in the Garden of Eden that are likely new to many of us.

Although the New Testament clearly connects Satan with the serpent in Genesis 3, it was actually a non-canonical text[19] that was the first to fully interpret the serpent as the devil. The Book of Wisdom was composed/compiled around 100 B.C. in Egypt. This Jewish text connects the fall of man with the devil himself.

> *Nevertheless through envy of the devil came death into the world: and they that do hold of his side do find it.*
> Wisdom 2:24 (KJV)

Following this, a later text gives an even more thorough depiction of Satan's involvement in the Garden of Eden. The Greek Life of Adam and Eve (which I think sounds like a fun sitcom where Adam and Eve live in Greece for a time) was possibly written sometime in the first century AD.[20] This was around the same

---

[19] See the glossary for more information. This text is considered non-canonical for Protestants. Likewise, even though it is a Jewish text, it is not considered canonical in Judaism. The Roman Catholic Church does consider the Book of Wisdom (or the Wisdom of Solomon) as part of its canon.

[20] There is debate among scholars regarding the time of composition for this work, ranging from first to fourth century AD. Pete Enns and John Levison, "Episode 269: Jack Levison - The Greek Life of Adam & Eve," The Bible For Normal People, April 22, 2024, https://thebiblefornormalpeople.com/episode-269-jack-levison-the-greek-life-of-adam-eve/.

time as the composition of the New Testament books. In this work from the Pseudepigrapha, we find an alleged conversation between the devil and the serpent.

> *And the devil spoke to the serpent, saying,*
> *"Get up. Come to me."*
> *And, having gotten up, he went to him.*
> *And the devil says to him,*
> *"I hear that you are shrewder than all the wild animals.*
> *<Listen to me> and I will talk with you.*
> *Why are you eating from the weeds of Adam and not*
> *from paradise? Get up and come, and let us make him to be*
> *thrown out of paradise, as also we were thrown out*
> *through him." The serpent says to him, "I am frightened*
> *that perhaps the Lord will be angry with me."*
> *The devil says to him, "Stop being frightened.*
> *Become a tool for me,*
> *and I myself will speak through your mouth*
> *one word aimed at deceiving them."* [21]

This text highlights a particular understanding of the serpent and Satan in Genesis 3—the serpent was coerced by Satan to do his bidding in the garden. This is a major step forward in the development of how readers interpreted and understood Genesis 3. Regrettably, we do not know if this is a strictly Jewish or a strictly Christian interpretation. There is considerable disagreement among scholars whether this text is Jewish or Christian in origin.[22]

Let's take a look at the Jewish interpretation of Genesis 3 in regard to the serpent and Satan. One special interpretation (or shall we say an enhanced, dramatic retelling) of the Genesis 3 narrative is found in the pseudepigraphal work called The Apocalypse of Abraham.[23] In this document, the Lord shows a vision of the

---

[21] John R. Levison, *The Greek Life of Adam and Eve* (Berlin: De Gruyter, 2023), 495.
[22] Levison, 85.
[23] Written sometime between 70 and 150 AD.

Garden of Eden to Abraham. Abraham sees Adam and Eve and another figure standing behind the tree from which they were eating. The figure is described in the text as "a serpent in form, having hands and feet like a man's, and wings on its shoulders, six on the right side and six on the left."[24] This is quite an eccentric and terrifying image of the serpent! This goes far beyond our normal thought of a serpent. The text goes on to elaborate the significance of this "serpent." The Lord says that this is he who "representeth ungodliness, their beginning (on the way) to perdition, even Azazel."[25] This particular rendering of the enemy in Genesis 3 paints a vivid picture of the serpent with hands, feet and wings. The serpent represents ungodliness and mankind's path to destruction. It does not go so far as to say that it was Satan himself or an instrument of Satan. As previously mentioned, there are understandings of Satan/the devil present in Jewish writings but these seem to fade away with the beginning of Rabbinic Judaism (that is, the more current form of Judaism following the destruction of the Second Temple). Indeed, the great enemy's role in Genesis 3 is typically not discussed in early Jewish rabbinical literature.[26]

Early rabbinical interpretation of Genesis 3 gives us Jewish understanding of the serpent in the early centuries AD. The views of the rabbis expressed in the Midrash have moved away from the serpent being under the influence (or represented by) Satan or a fallen angel to a focus on the uniqueness and intelligence of the serpent. Elaine Phillips writes, "The rabbis gave to the serpent a malevolent personality but one that functioned on the level of a very clever, logical, and articulate human being."[27] Like an evil Disney cartoon character, the serpent is viewed as able to walk, talk, and manipulate. One particular Rabbi insinuates that the serpent's intelligence was comparable to the Lord's:

With Adam He had a discussion, with Eve He had a discussion, but with the serpent, He did not have any

---

[24] G. H. Box and J Landsman, eds., *The Apocalypse of Abraham*, 2nd ed. (New York: MacMillan, 1919), Chapter 23.

[25] Box and Landsman, *The Apocalypse of Abraham*, Chapter 23.

[26] Grypeou and Spurling, *The Book of Genesis in Late Antiquity*, 88.

[27] Phillips, "Serpent Intertexts," 243.

<blockquote>

discussion. Rather, the Holy One blessed be He said: "This serpent is a wicked one, with all the answers. If I say something to it, now it will say to me: You commanded them, and I commanded them. Why did they forsake your command and follow my command?" Instead, He summarily issued his sentence.[28]

</blockquote>

In addition to the snake's superb intelligence, the Jewish Midrash offers thoughts on what the serpent was like before his curse. Rabbi Hoshaya Rabba says that the serpent stood up tall and had legs. Also, Rabbi Shimon ben Elazar theorizes that the serpent was said to be "like a camel. The world lost a great benefit, as were it not so [that the serpent was punished], man would have been able to send merchandise with it and it would have been able to come and go [by itself]."[29] Another rabbinic viewpoint is that when the Lord pronounced his curse upon the serpent, His angels descended and removed the arms and legs from the serpent as well as its voice. A further interpretation is that the Lord removed the serpent's ability to walk and eat like a man.[30] All in all, we find the early rabbinic Jewish faith emphasizing the serpent's special qualities and pre-curse form. In general, Satan as the great enemy of God (and not simply as the accuser as we have seen) is not involved in Genesis 3 and has no connections with the serpent. This is especially true as Jewish faith progresses. Even today, Jewish belief holds the doctrine of Satan as an accuser, but not as the devil—the ultimate entity against the Lord.[31] For the Jewish reader, therefore, the serpent does not mean or represent the devil.

How was the serpent understood and interpreted in the early centuries of Christianity? We have already seen how the New Testament brings us to an

---

[28] Bereshit Rabbah 20:2.

[29] Bereshit Rabbah 19:1. Imagine the ancient world with large serpents being used for transportation instead of camels and donkeys.

[30] Bereshit Rabbah 20:5

[31] https://whatjewsbelieve.org/there-is-the-satan-but-not-the-devil/. This is a good website that provides a simple yet articulate belief about mainstream Judaism today.

interpretation of the serpent being equated with Satan. Beyond that, how was the serpent/Satan connection understood?

In contrast to traditional Jewish thought, early Christians generally did not view the serpent as capable of bringing about the transgression of Eve and Adam.[32] The serpent itself was not responsible for its cunning and deceitful actions, but another entity was responsible for it. The early suggestion, which was already alluded to through New Testament verses, was that God's Adversary, Satan, was responsible for the fall. Indeed, that is the instance of the Humpty Dumpty Effect that I have written about. There are multiple approaches to understanding *how* Satan interacted/caused the serpent to bring about the fall of man, but the most common approach was that he used the serpent (intermediary or instrument) but was not the serpent itself.[33]

There are some variations in early Christian interpretation and understandings of the serpent and Satan in the Genesis 3 account. John Chrysostom explains that Satan saw that the serpent was an intelligent beast, able to communicate with man and thus used the creature to deceive the woman.[34] In a similar vein, Severian of Gabala emphasizes the serpent's high intelligence; he even suggests that before the fall serpents would serve as companions with humans similarly to dogs. His writing is worth quoting. He explains: "Before the fall, Adam was filled with wisdom, discernment and prophecy. . .When the devil noticed the snake's intelligence and Adam's high opinion of it (Adam considered the snake very wise), the devil spoke through the snake so that Adam would think that the snake, being intelligent, was able to imitate even human speech."[35] In this sense, the devil used the serpent as his instrument to communicate. Likewise, John of Damascus argues that serpents

---

[32] Grypeou and Spurling, *The Book of Genesis in Late Antiquity*, 69.

[33] Grypeou and Spurling, 87.

[34] John Chrysostom, Homilies on Genesis 16.3.

[35] Thomas C. Oden and Andrew Louth, eds., *Ancient Christian Commentary on Scripture. Old Testament: Vol. 1: Genesis 1-11*, vol. 1 (Downers Grove, IL: InterVarsity Press, 2001), 74-75. Severian falsely notes that the serpent spoke with Adam, not Eve. Read your Bible, Severian!

and man were on intimate terms and could speak with one another. Because of their closeness, the devil utilized the serpent's relationship to do his bidding.[36]

In Milton's Paradise Lost, Satan finds a serpent to use to tempt man.
Illustration by Gustave Doré, 1866.

Another early Church Father, Didymus the Blind[37], held the belief that the serpent in Genesis 3 was the devil. Living and writing in the 300s AD, Didymus asserts that it was the devil in the garden that tricked the woman (Eve).[38] Didymus the Blind[39] did not view the serpent as being able to talk and be rational on its own. He writes, "It is clear, however, that it is not this serpent to which God applies retribution; it was not naturally able to proffer deceitful words that would

---

[36] Oden and Louth, 75.

[37] I don't know if he was given this title post-mortem, while he was alive, or before he was born. If either of the first two are correct, maybe we should just use a surname instead of picking on him for a physical disability. If the third, his parents must have had excellent "foresight."

[38] Didymus the Blind, *Fathers of the Church: A New Translation. Commentary on Genesis*, trans. Robert Hill (Catholic University of America Press, 2016), 94.

[39] I propose we call him Didymus the Great.

encourage God to inflict retribution on it."[40] Didymus later comments regarding the punishment, adding that it was not a serpent but "'the serpent,' thus suggesting the devil is person who is responsible for evil in others as well."[41] Furthermore, Didymus elaborates, "Surpassing everything that has the savagery of vice, the devil under the name *serpent* consequently receives a condemnation beyond all."[42]

The famous Saint Augustine succinctly states that the serpent signifies the devil. He also argues that the serpent was not literally/physically in the garden of Eden but was present only spiritually. Thus, Augustine attributes the deceit to the devil and his schemes.[43] Altogether, we find that the early Church Fathers viewed the serpent and his deceit as the work of God's Adversary, the devil. The specific method may vary, but the source is still the same. Many early commentators in the Christian tradition also noted the uniqueness of the serpent pre-fall, yet whatever intelligence, form, or abilities the serpent had before the curse were insufficient to bring about the damaging results of sin.

---

[40] Didymus the Blind, 94.

[41] Didymus the Blind, 95

[42] Didymus the Blind, 95.

[43] Oden and Louth, *Ancient Christian Commentary,* 76.

As you can see, there are differing interpretations and understandings of the serpent in Genesis 3 for Jewish and Christian readers. For the Jewish reader, the serpent is not an instrument or intermediary for Satan but is generally viewed as an intelligent animal. For the Christian reader, the source behind the serpent's cunning is Satan himself. Why the different understandings of the same Text? The Christian reads this story through the interpretive lens of the New Testament. Through the teaching on the devil in the New Testament, coupled with other Christian doctrines, the Christian will read Genesis 3 and understand the serpent and meaning of the passage in a different way than the Jewish reader (who does not believe in the inspiration of the New Testament or Jesus as Divine). Following this chapter is a subsection on interpretive differences of the Old Testament between Jews and Christians. It is very insightful about biblical interpretation and how our respective backgrounds influence how we read the Text.

Just like the apple as the forbidden fruit, viewing the serpent as Satan in the Garden of Eden is an example of the Humpty Dumpty Effect. Yet, unlike the apple interpretation, interpreting the serpent as Satan is a valid interpretative method for the Christian. It is not improper to do so because the New Testament Scriptures support and encourage such a reading (interpreting Scripture with Scripture). So, the next time your Sunday School class is discussing Genesis 3, and someone refers to the serpent as Satan—let it slide; it's all good. But if they refer to the forbidden fruit as an apple, correct them in love and proceed to throw grapes at them.

Differences in Interpretation of OT texts between Christians and Jews

When a person goes to read the Bible, he or she intrinsically brings assumptions, preconceived notions, and a specific worldview to the Text. One may say that each reader of the Bible carries an interpretive lens through which the Text is read. While my goal in this book is not to take the reader into a deep dive into the world of biblical hermeneutics[44], some discussion of the art of interpretation is necessary. This interpretive lens is held by the reader and helps to form our meaning of the Text, much in the same way that we have assumed that Humpty Dumpty was an egg.

Both Christians and Jews carry their own respective interpretive lenses when they read the Holy Scriptures. We have examined a portion of Genesis chapter 3 in detail in this book. While this passage is the same for both Jewish and Christian readers, they walk away with different interpretations and understandings of this

---

[44] Included in my provided glossary. As a reminder, hermeneutics is the study or method of interpretation; it is often used in speaking of interpreting the Bible. The word originates from the Greek word for interpretation. When a husband reads but fails to interpret his wife's written message, it's called Hismeneutics.

sacred Text. For the Jewish reader, the serpent in Genesis 3 was crafty and tempted Eve; for the Christian reader, the source behind the temptation was ultimately Satan himself. Same text, but different interpretations of it. There is a major interpretive difference for both Jews and Christians readers that arises out of this passage—the doctrine of original sin. When Christians read Genesis 3, they find the fundamental Text for this doctrine. Because Adam and Eve sinned, all future descendants of mankind have an inherent sinfulness and guilt.[45] Yet, when the Jewish reader comes to Genesis 3, they do not walk away with the doctrine of original sin. Rabbi Joseph Telushkin writes that "original sin does not occupy an important place in [conventional] Jewish theology…the prevailing attitude among Jewish scholars is that people sin *as* Adam and Eve sinned, not *because* they sinned."[46]

Why the different interpretations? When Christians read Genesis 3, they read it from the perspective of Paul's writings and how the New Testament frames this narrative. Furthermore, Christians will read into it their own faith tradition's particular stance on original sin. Conversely, the Jewish reader does not consider what the New Testament says in interpreting Genesis.

This phenomenon is not isolated to this passage in Genesis but could easily apply to many passages in the Old Testament/Tanakh. Even something that we may consider simple or straightforward can lead to interpretation variations or difficulties. One example would be the Sixth Commandment: "You shall not murder."[47] Yet, early English translations of the Bible (1599 Geneva Bible and the King James Version) have the Sixth Commandment as "Thou shalt not kill." While to some people it may splitting hairs, there is an important distinction between murdering and killing. To murder is to take the life of another intentionally and unlawfully, while to kill is to simply take another's life regardless

---

[45] See Romans 5:12-21 for a Pauline focus on this doctrine. Also, it is summed up nicely in 1 Cor. 15:22: "For as in Adam all die, so in Christ all will be made alive."

[46] Joseph Telushkin, *Biblical Literacy: The Most Important People, Events, and Ideas of the Hebrew Bible* (New York: HarperCollins, 2002), 10.

[47] Exodus 20:13 NIV. Standard Jewish translations follow the same interpretation.

of the context.[48] The Sixth Commandment has generally been understood (and translated) as the prohibition against murder, not killing. Likewise, the Jewish interpretation follows this same practice. This makes sense on account of two main things. First, the Hebrew language contains separate words for murdering and killing. רָצַח/ratsach is the Hebrew word for murder, while the word for kill is הָרַג/harag. If the commandment intended to forbid any type of killing, lawful or unlawful, the Hebrew word harag would have been used in the commandment as opposed to ratsach. Second, to read the Old Testament/Tanakh completely is to understand that the Sixth Commandment cannot legitimately mean a prohibition against any killing. There are way too many instances where there would be a contradiction in the Text. Consider the times when the Lord ordains capital punishment for certain offenders…or the times when the Lord leads His people into battle.[49] Also, Exodus 22:2 pardons the person who takes the life of another that breaks into his house at night. The Old Testament would be very much contradicting itself if it forbade any killing while at the same time pardoning or ordaining it on some occasions.

Why do some early translations (and some people's thoughts) have the Sixth Commandment as forbidding killing and not murder? One theory has to do with Jesus' teaching in the New Testament. When you consider the entirety of Jesus' teaching, His message appears to be against violence. Consider these verses.

> *You have heard that it was said, "Eye for eye, and tooth for tooth." But I tell you, do not resist an evil person.*
> *If anyone slaps you on the right cheek,*
> *turn to them the other cheek also.*
> (Matthew 5:38-39)
> *"Put your sword back in its place," Jesus said to him,*
> *"for all who draw the sword will die by the sword."*
> (Matthew 26:52)

---

[48] Think of involuntary manslaughter or a killing in self-defense as examples.
[49] Telushkin, 433-434.

A cursory reading of these verses shows that Jesus was not in favor of violence. It is speculated that the anti-violence teaching of Christ informed the early translations of the Sixth Commandment. Furthermore, Rabbi Joseph Telushkin theorizes that early Bible translators sought to make the Sixth Commandment consistent with Jesus' teaching on violence. Thus, they translated the Sixth Commandment as "kill" instead of "murder" so there would not be any contradiction with what Jesus said.[50] Even today, people still mix up the words in the commandment.

The final example I want to consider is the Messianic prophecies in the Old Testament. There are many instances in the New Testament where an Old Testament Text is quoted or alluded to as fulfillment of a prophecy. The early Christian movement saw the proclamation of the Gospel as a continuation of what God had been doing in the history of the Israelites. The New Testament writers aim to show a continuation of God's work—Old Covenant and New Covenant. Biblical scholars Joel Green and Richard Hays comment on this by writing: "Their fundamental conviction was that God had acted in an unexpected way to fulfill the promises made to Israel, to bring to completion the whole history of God's dealing with this people. With transformed eyes, they read and reread Scripture, discovering there prefigurations of the grace of God they had come to experience."[51] In short, the writers of the New Testament show that the Old Testament texts anticipated the Gospel and the events in the New Testament.

The Christian, armed with the New Testament, will approach the Old Testament differently than a Jewish person without the New Testament. As an example, let us consider two well-known passages from the Old Testament book of Isaiah. The first is found in Isaiah 7:10-14 concerning the arrival of *Immanuel.*

---

[50] Telushkin, xxvii. Telushkin also suggests that improvement in the Hebrew language by Christian scholars led to the correction in translating the Sixth Commandment.
[51] Joel B. Green and Richard B. Hays, "The Use of the Old Testament by New Testament Writers," essay, in *Hearing the New Testament: Strategies for Interpretation,* ed. Joel B. Green (Grand Rapids, Mich: W.B. Eerdmans Pub. Co, 2010), 122–39, 123. This chapter is a good resource for further insight on this topic.

<blockquote>
Again the Lord spoke to Ahaz,
"Ask the Lord your God for a sign,
whether in the deepest depths or in the highest heights."
But Ahaz said, "I will not ask;
I will not put the Lord to the test."
Then Isaiah said, "Hear now, you house of David! Is it not enough to try the patience of humans? Will you try the patience of my God also? Therefore the Lord himself will give you a sign: The virgin will conceive and give birth to a son, and will call him Immanuel.
</blockquote>

The main takeaway from this Text varies greatly between Jewish readers and Christian readers. The Jewish reader sees no reference to Jesus at all…only a prophetic sign given to obstinate King Ahaz who refuses to trust in the Lord. Yet the Christian reads "Immanuel" and interprets it as a foreshadowing of Jesus' birth to the Virgin Mary. The proper way to understand the Text is to understand that there is both a meaning in its original context surrounding King Ahaz and a Messianic prophecy as well.

Let's consider the Text in more detail. One sticky issue is the translation of the Hebrew word עַלְמָה/'almah. While the NIV (and many other Christian translations including the KJV and the Geneva Bible) interpret it as "virgin," it is more accurate to translate it as "young woman."[52] (Jewish translations such as the JPS 2023 and the Complete Jewish Bible render it as "young woman.") Now, a young woman may be a virgin, but not necessarily so. If Isaiah wanted to convey 100% the status of the lady in question, he could have used the Hebrew word בְּתוּלָה/ bethulah which means virgin.[53] Some Jewish readers take this as a reason for why this text is not a prophecy for Jesus.

---

[52] Remember in the previous section about the translation of the Sixth Commandment? Something similar is going on here. Hang tight! It will be explained.

[53] Telushkin, *Biblical Literacy,* 288.

So, what's going on in this Text? King Ahaz is the King of Judah at this time. The northern tribes of Israel along with Aram attempt to seize Judah but are unsuccessful. Regardless, King Ahaz is shaken. Whom shall he trust? Where is his strength? Will he trust in the Lord or turn to the Assyrian empire for help against his enemies? The Lord tells Ahaz to ask for a sign so that he knows that the Lord is with him and the nation of Judah. Yet, Ahaz refuses. But God says He will give him a sign regardless of asking or not. The sign is as we read in the passage: the young woman/virgin will be with child…

Is Isaiah 7 a prophecy about Jesus or is it a prophetic sign for Judah at that point in history? I would argue (along with many others) that it is both. The prophets gave many signs from the Lord—a child being named "Immanuel" would by no means be the strangest one (just ask Hosea!). The Lord is showing Ahaz and the people of Judah that He is with them, and they do not need to run to other nations for help.

Despite the original context and meaning, Christians predominantly view this Text as a Messianic prophecy. This is largely because of what we find in the New Testament. The Gospel of Matthew quotes part of Isaiah 7:14 connecting Jesus' birth with the Isaiah text.

> *All this took place to fulfill what the Lord had said through the prophet: "The virgin will conceive and give birth to a son, and they will call him Immanuel"*
> *(which means "God with us").*
> (Matthew 1:22-23)

It is noteworthy to mention that the Septuagint, the Greek translation of the Old Testament, translates עַלְמָה/l'almah as *parthenos,* meaning virgin. If Matthew uses the Septuagint as his starting point, it makes sense why he would continue to use the same word, parthenos/virgin, in 1:22, thus fulfilling the prophecy and showing Jesus as the promised Messiah to come.

Since Matthew's Gospel has given us this insight on the Isaiah 7:14 passage, it is hard for Christians to look at the passage with its original meaning and context. Consequently, when a Christian translator looks at Isaiah 7:14, it is natural to view it as the passage Matthew quotes in supporting the virgin birth of Jesus. Thus, we have the natural tendency to translate it as "virgin" instead of "young woman" even though the latter is a more accurate translation of the Hebrew. It helps to remember that biblical translation never happens in a vacuum. Matthew likely cites Isaiah 7:14 because of the Septuagint's rendering of עַלְמָה/'almah as virgin.[54] William Tyndale, in translating the Greek New Testament into English, uses the term "repentance" instead of "penance" because of the negative connotations with Roman Catholic Church's penitential exercises during the Medieval time period.[55] Similar examples abound!

Some modern scholars have accused Matthew of misconstruing Isaiah's message to fit his narrative. That's not the case. Matthew was inspired by the Holy Spirit and was led to share God's prophetic sign from Isaiah 7 and apply it to Jesus' birth. In his commentary on Isaiah, John Goldingay refers to Matthew's use of Isaiah as "inspired *re*applications of the inspired words."[56] I find that to be an accurate description of what happens when the New Testament authors quote the Old Testament. John Oswalt, Old Testament Professor and Scholar, refers to Isaiah's prophetic sign as a single meaning with double significance.[57] How true is that! This single sign for Isaiah's original audience meant something for them then; it also signifies the coming of the Messiah who forever abides with us.[58]

The second example of a Messianic prophecy in the Old Testament is found in Isaiah 52:13-53:12. This section, commonly titled as "The Suffering Servant," is

---

[54] John Barton, *The Word: How We Translate the Bible-and Why It Matters* (New York: Basic Books, 2023), 260-261. This is a really good book if you want to dive into understanding biblical translation. Barton does an awesome job of highlighting some wonderful ideas with translation...more wonderful than the donut I just consumed. It would have been better without the stale, pink frosting.
[55] Barton, 18.
[56] John Goldingay, *Isaiah* (Grand Rapids, Mich: Baker Books, 2012), 67.
[57] John N. Oswalt, Isaiah (Grand Rapids, MI: Zondervan Academic, 2010). EBSCOhost.
[58] Professor Oswalt offers a superb discussion of this section of Isaiah and discussion on this topic. You should check it out—after you finish reading this book. :)

viewed differently from the perspectives of Christians and Jews. Because of its length, I won't quote the entire section but just share two prominent verses for us to get the gist of the passage.

> *But he was pierced for our transgressions,*
> *he was crushed for our iniquities;*
> *the punishment that brought us peace was on him,*
> *and by his wounds we are healed.*
> (Isaiah 53:5)
> *He was oppressed and afflicted,*
> *yet he did not open his mouth;*
> *he was led like a lamb to the slaughter,*
> *and as a sheep before its shearers is silent,*
> *so he did not open his mouth.*
> (Isaiah 53:7)

Who is this suffering servant that the passage is talking about? Popular Jewish interpretations view the suffering servant as either being the prophet Isaiah himself or the entire Jewish people.[59] There is nothing wrong with either of these interpretations. Isaiah was a faithful servant of the Lord who suffered during his prophetic ministry. Likewise, there are references in the book of Isaiah where God's people, the Jewish nation, are referred to as the Lord's servant.[60]

The overwhelmingly popular Christian interpretation of this Text is that it is foreshadowing the suffering and death of Jesus Christ. Similar to the situation with Matthew's treatment of Isaiah 7:14, a scene in the New Testament book of Acts sets the stage for future Christian understanding of Isaiah 52-53. Philip the

---

59 Telushkin, Biblical Literacy, 289.

[60] Telushkin, 289. Rabbi Telushkin also elucidates that this section of Isaiah has traditionally been understood as "referring to the Jewish people's sufferings while trying to maintain their faith and make the idea of One God known to the world."

deacon[61] encounters a man who is reading Isaiah and is having trouble comprehending it. Philip connects Isaiah 53 with Jesus' atoning sacrifice.

> *The eunuch asked Philip, "Tell me, please, who is the prophet talking about, himself or someone else?" Then Philip began with that very passage of Scripture and told him the good news about Jesus.*
> (Acts 8:34-35)

When the Christian reads this passage in Isaiah and compares it with what Jesus went through, it is obvious that Isaiah was prophesying about the Messiah. The Apostle Peter, through the Spirit's inspiration saw the same thing and thus refers to the Isaiah 53 passage multiple times in 1 Peter chapter 2.[62] Thus, while the Jewish reader views the suffering servant as referring to either Isaiah himself or the Jewish people collectively, the Christian reader views it as a prophecy for Jesus.

The reader views the Text with his or her interpretive lens. Both Christians and Jews will view the Old Testament/Tanakh with this lens. May we as followers of Jesus learn to look at not just the Text through this lens but the entire world.

---

[61] This Philip is often referred to as "Philip the deacon" or "Philip the evangelist" in order to distinguish him from Philip who was an apostle of Jesus.
[62] 1 Peter 2:22-25.

CHAPTER 4: THE RELATIONSHIP BETWEEN DAVID AND JONATHAN

Manuscript illustration of David and Jonathan.
La Somme le roy circa 1300 AD.

In recent years, I have found myself eschewing music on the radio in favor of podcasts and audiobooks. Audiobooks are my jam. I end up spending a lot of time driving kids to and from school, going to appointments and to church functions (and getting coffee of course). Going on a trip that would take several hours in the car, I needed to find a good audiobook to help the drive be less boring. I stumbled upon *The Secret Chord* by Geraldine Brooks. The book is a piece of historical fiction about King David. Since King David is pretty cool,[1] I thought I would give it a try. Realizing that this was historical fiction, I expected there to be some creative liberties as the author filled in the gaps in the life of King David. What I did not expect was Brooks' portrayal of the relationship between David and Jonathan as a sexual relationship. I must confess that when this was introduced into the storyline, I quit listening. This element of the story bothered me—why would anyone think of portraying these two characters as having that sort of a relationship? At first blush, it seemed way off base and a huge distortion of the narrative of Scripture.

You may be surprised to learn that this book's depiction of King David having a homosexual relationship with Jonathan is not the first occurrence of such an idea. Not even close! I will say more than on that shortly. It has become commonplace for people to view the nature of the relationship between David and Jonathan as more than just friends but as sexual lovers. The origin of such an interpretation stems from a few passages of Scripture in 1 and 2 Samuel wherein the language is vague and not easily understood in our current cultural context. We will examine the Scriptures concerned later on in this section. Now, I simply bring to the reader's attention how this example of interpreting the text has grown…It has become another Humpty Dumpty. Biblical scholar James Harding has written the work, *The Love of David and Jonathan: Ideology, Text, Reception*, which is in my opinion the best resource available on this debate right now. Harding writes on this ever-widening interpretation of 1 and 2 Samuel: "The idea that the relationship between David and Jonathan was sexual has, in fact, become commonplace, so much so that the very mention of David and Jonathan can be

---

[1] Citation needed??? Probably not. David is awesome.

shorthand for a gay relationship."[2] In this section, I shall share with the reader the modern instances of this Humpty Dumpty Effect, briefly tracing its history of interpretation. Next, we will look closer at the relevant Scripture passages that have led to this interpretation of David and Jonathan's relationship, while briefly learning some traditional approaches to the Text. Lastly, I will share some alternative understandings of David and Jonathan's relationship.

It is important for me to offer some remarks on this section. My original plan for this book consisted of writing two sections from the Old Testament (the ones from Genesis) and two from the New Testament; this section was not planned. When I learned of this common interpretation of David and Jonathan, I instantly saw how it fit into my book's thesis. I did have an internal debate on whether or not to include this section because of its mature subject matter and the controversial nature of homosexuality in the Christian Church today. I thought of young readers such as my sons—would they be overwhelmed by this topic? Or would it be inappropriate for them? Perhaps. Yet, I concluded that it would be better to write and allow the reader to decide, or if necessary to skip over it. Readers who are able to digest the other content of this book are likely at the age where they can tackle this discussion.

Also, I was tempted not to include this section because of the tension that exists in the Church today surrounding issues related to alternative sexuality. I did not want to ostracize those who may disagree with me on this perspective. Obviously, I decided to keep it here. I would hope that a reader can deal with me even if she disagrees with something. Respectful and loving dialogue is needed both in the Church and in the world today. Currently, there is a lot of division in church denominations over how to relate to LGBTQ persons. Are such lifestyles sinful or permissible? Should they be allowed into membership? Should they be allowed to serve? Can they be ordained? I belong to the Church of the Nazarene, a denomination in the Wesleyan-Arminian tradition, which declares that

---

[2] James E. Harding, *The Love of David and Jonathan: Ideology, Text, Reception* (London: Routledge, Taylor & Francis Group, 2013), 3.

homosexual behavior is contrary to God's will.[3] I agree with the denomination's official stance on the matter and do not shy away from it. But I do wish to emphasize the Church's responsibility to be loving, hospitable, and respectful to all people. I hope the reader will agree with my latter statement. The aim of this book is not to debate sexuality in the Church, nor is it designed to be an exhaustive scholarly approach to sexuality in the Bible. My focus is on the debated Texts featuring David and Jonathan and how they are received and interpreted. Because of this, I do not plan to use certain words or phrases regarding the nature of David and Jonathan's relationship. Rather, I shall simply refer to the proposed nature of their relationship as a "sexual relationship."[4]

While not as popular as Adam and Eve, King David has served as a prominent figure for both Jews and Christian for well over two millennia. David's resume is no small thing: he is widely regarded as Israel's greatest king, known as a man after God's own heart, and in the ancestral line of Jesus. David's name and legacy is an ongoing theme for both the Old and New Testaments. Because of his prominence in the Christian faith, many were shocked by some comments made in 2011 on BBC Radio. The year 2011 marked the 400th anniversary of the King James Bible. To celebrate the anniversary of one of the most widely known publications of all time, the BBC held a radio program featuring biblical readings and commentary. In the program, English playwright Howard Brenton accused King David of being homosexual. He stated on the radio: "To a secular reader the story of David and

---

[3] Manual statement on same sex relations: "Because we believe that it is God's intention for our sexuality to be lived out in the covenantal union between one woman and one man, we believe the practice of same-sex sexual intimacy is contrary to God's will for human sexuality. While a person's homosexual or bi-sexual attraction may have complex and differing origins, and the implication of this call to sexual purity is costly, we believe the grace of God is sufficient for such a calling. We recognize the shared responsibility of the body of Christ to be a **welcoming**, **forgiving**, and **loving** community where hospitality, encouragement, transformation, and accountability are available to all." Bold words are mine.
Church of the Nazarene Manual 2023 (Kansas City: The Foundry Publishing, 2024), 56.
[4] I am setting aside any concern of "sexual orientation" for David and Jonathan (homosexual or bisexual). Also, I am avoiding terms such as homoerotic and gay. For simplicity, I am calling the interpretation of their relationship as a "sexual relationship" without defining it further.

Jonathan's love is obviously homosexual, the only gay relationship in the Bible"[5]
The response, which reached millions of people on one of the most listened to
radio stations in the world, was shocking. Many likely heard this theory of David
and Jonathan's relationship for the first time. Yet, this is hardly the only
proclamation of this interpretation of King David's sexuality.

I have already shared Geraldine Brooks' depiction of David and Jonathan but there
are many other instances of this interpretation. The movie *Death at a Funeral*
contains one of the oft-debated passages about David's relationship with Jonathan
(1 Samuel 18:1-4). A connection is made in the movie between David and
Jonathan's sexual relationship with that of a secret homosexual relationship
between two of the movie's characters. In 2008, the crime show *Silent Witness*
worked with the understanding that Jonathan and David were engaged in an erotic
relationship.[6] Other movies and films depict David and Jonathan (either explicitly
or at least hinting) as having a sexual relationship. These include the 1985 movie
King David and the 2009 NBC show *Kings*. It remains to be seen how the 2025
show *House of David* will depict their relationship. Also, the 1972 novel *The King
David Report* portrays David as having a sexual relationship with Jonathan. The
depictions of this interpretation aren't just found in media but in real life
discussions, including political debates. One example would be when the Israeli
parliament, the Knesset, was debating gay rights and the relationship between
David and Jonathan was brought into the conversation. Likewise, when civil
unions for same-sex couples were being discussed in Vermont, it was argued that
David and Jonathan had a homosexual relationship.

This interpretation of David and Jonathan has been widespread in recent decades,
but how far back does it go? When did people start to think of the two men in this
manner? How did it get here? The development of this particular interpretation is
connected with a general movement of the world with embracing alternative
sexuality, a growing secular approach to biblical studies, and interpretations of

---

[5] "Audio: BBC Mars Anniversary of KJV Bible with Gay Slur," The Christian Institute,
January 17, 2011, https://www.christian.org.uk/news/audio-bbc-mars-400th-
anniversary-of-kjv-bible-with-gay-slur/.
[6] Harding, *The Love of David and Jonathan*, 6.

Paria Amicorum (you thought we were done with the Latin, didn't you?). During the Renaissance Period (roughly 14th to 17th centuries), there existed a renewed emphasis on friendship.[7] The Renaissance Period also had a "rediscovery" of classical writings and the Greek and Roman roots for European culture.[8] With friendship, classical writings, and Greek history being important to this movement, we find in Renaissance literature many references to ancient friendships as examples of great companionship. Writing about paria amicorum, Latin for "pair of friends," was common within Renaissance literature. Male friends from Greek and Roman literature and history were shared as paria amicorum. Examples would be Hercules and Hylas, Schilles and Patroclus, and Socrates and Alcibiades.[9] In time, the friendship pairing of David and Jonathan started to appear alongside these Greek/Roman pairs of friends.

Now, there is nothing wrong with listing David and Jonathan alongside these paria amicorum. In fact, we even find at least a couple Renaissance pieces of literature with a Christian focus that exalt David and Jonathan above the usual paria amicorum.[10] Cool beans. The dynamic changes when a philosopher provides a new interpretation on the Bible and the paria amicorum begin to be viewed in a different way.

Jeremy Bentham (1748-1832) was an English philosopher; he is regarded as the father of utilitarianism. He rejected the Church early in his life and was an atheist. Despite his atheism and disdain for organized religion, he still would study the Bible and give his own interpretation of it from a secular point of view. In arguing for England to relax the laws that prohibited homosexual relationships, he surprisingly turned to the Bible for justification. Bentham writes that the relationship between David and Jonathan was not simply one of friendship or "mind to mind" but was indeed sexual—"body to body."[11] This is the first explicit

---

[7] That's the only boat that can never sink. A Friend-ship.

[8] Harding, 282.

[9] BTW, all of these names were vetoed by my wife for our boys' names.

[10] *Loci Communes* (1576) and *Davideis* (1712).

[11] Philip Schofield, "Jeremy Bentham: Prophet of Secularism," Journal of Bentham Studies, September 17, 2024, https://journals.uclpress.co.uk/jbs/article/id/3260/.

reference to David and Jonathan having a sexual relationship.[12] You should also be aware that Bentham held some crazy interpretations in regards to sexuality—he believed that Jesus had a sexual relationship with the Beloved Disciple (John). Furthermore, he argued that it was possible that Jesus had sexual relations with other male disciples and some females.[13]

Another significant factor that affected the interpretation of David and Jonathan's relationship is the renewed focus on Plato's literature in the 1800s. I dare not dive into Plato's literature for fear of putting the reader and me to sleep, but suffice it to say that there exists in some of his literature discussions of pederasty and other forms of love. Rather than understanding the pederastic relationship in Plato's literature as referring to a spiritual or deep friendship, the interpretation shifted so that it was mainly viewed as physical, sexual expression. Alongside this reading of Plato, other older works of literature, including the lists of paria amicorum, came to be seen through the lens of homosexuality instead of simply friendship.[14] Thus, we find a new way of looking at David and Jonathan, inspired by cultural, literary, and societal influences far removed from the biblical Text.

---

[12] Lord Byron refers to David and Jonathan in literature, but his writing is murky on how he understands their relationship. With Bentham's writing in the early 1800s we have no doubt.

[13] Schofield, section 6.

[14] Harding, *The Love of David and Jonathan*, 289. Again, Harding follows this interpretive trail in great detail. Harding also comments in the conclusion of his book on page 403: "There exists a reading convention that sees 'David and Jonathan' as a reference to a gay relationship, a convention that evolved under the influence of a very complex network of ideological struggles and reading strategies in the nineteenth century."

Portrait of Irish poet and playwright Oscar Wilde. On trial for homosexual activities in 1895, he refers to the "the love that dare not speak its name." He stated that David and Jonathan were an example of this love.

The increasing popularity of interpreting David and Jonathan as such has led to its inclusion in what is known as a "gay canon," a collection of literature representing the homosexual community. A modern example of this would be the book *The Columbia Anthology of Gay Literature*. In such an established collection, you would find literature from many regions of the world and different time periods but all with the same assumption that there are homosexual characters in the story.[15] Such an inclusion reinforces this particular interpretation of David and Jonathan-just as we continue to think of Humpty Dumpty as an egg because we see it so often. Similar to this, we find this interpretation commonly espoused in the hermeneutic known as "queer reading." Professor of Biblical Studies Markus

---

[15] Although such works may not explicitly state the characters are homosexual or engaged in activity, one has to assume that an inclusion in such a collection of literature would lead the reader to make that interpretation.

Zehnder writes regarding those who take this interpretive approach to David and Jonathan and other literature: "the adherents of a so-called queer reading, who take their own homosexual self-identification or experiences as the starting point of their reading and interpreting of biblical texts."[16] It is common for there to be various approaches to literature in our modern setting, and such a queer reading is one example. Yet, this sort of approach is troublesome as it can be viewed as contradicting the Text itself. You wouldn't read a Dr. Seuss book looking for insights on quantum physics, so why would you read the Tanakh looking for homosexuality?[17] Yet, those who embrace such an approach to the Text would argue otherwise. This raises some interesting and challenging questions for us: who owns the Text? Who gets to say how it is used or what it means?

Who owns the Text?

Here is a challenging question to consider: who owns the Bible?

Obvious answers may be "God" or "the Church," but even if those answers are in some sense correct, it still leaves us with more challenging questions and quandaries.[18]

In modern-day literature, written works are copyrighted©. This demonstrates who is the author or owner of a work. If there is a question about ownership or interpretation, we know where to look for answers. For example, if I write a book (I guess that's true…) and someone is unsure about what I wrote, he or she can ask me to explain.

---

[16] Markus Zehnder, "Observations on the Relationship between David and Jonathan and the Debate on Homosexuality," *The Westminster Theological Journal* 69, no. 1 (2007): 127–74, 129.

[17] Especially as parts of the Mosaic Law prohibit homosexual activities (see Lev. 18:22).

[18] The Bible is inspired by the Lord but given to the world. God is the main author of the Text, but we don't hold specific confirmation on its meaning. To claim that the Church owns the Bible is difficult—the Church universal? A specific local church or denomination? The Church as a whole may, let's say, own interpretive rights for the Bible but the whole Church doesn't agree. Likewise, there would be a lot of discussion on who's in and who's out when it comes to clarifying the Church.

While there are specific versions of the Bible, and countless numbers of commentaries, studies, and other books based on the Bible that are copyrighted, the Bible itself is not. The divinely inspired 66 books that compose the canon are available to be read and used by all. The individual authors who wrote the books of the Bible are no longer with us and thus are not available for questioning ☹.

The difficult truth is that nobody really "owns" the Bible (contrary to a recent social media rumor that the Walt Disney Company bought the rights to the Bible). It is God's revelation to the world that instructs us about Him and how we are to live. Since the Bible has no exact "owner," it can be misused. It is frustrating when people misuse words of the Holy Scriptures. Encouraging people to be honest with the Text is a good start—not falling into the temptation of cherry-picking verses out of context or trying to make a verse mean something it clearly does not mean.[19] Ultimately, there is great accountability and judgment for all of us with how we treat the Holy Scriptures.

---

[19] A running joke in my family is that Revelation 8:1 proves there will be no women in Heaven. Of course, we never seriously teach that. If we did, that would be bad, and it would be an example of how not to use Scripture.

Let us now look at the biblical passages that are often connected with this interpretation of David and Jonathan.[20]

> ### 1 Samuel 18:1-4
> *After David had finished talking with Saul, Jonathan became one in spirit with David, and he loved him as himself. From that day Saul kept David with him and did not let him return home to his family. And Jonathan made a covenant with David because he loved him as himself. Jonathan took off the robe he was wearing and gave it to David, along with his tunic, and even his sword, his bow and his belt.*
>
> ### 1 Samuel 19:1-2
> *Saul told his son Jonathan and all the attendants to kill David. But Jonathan had taken a great liking to David and warned him…*
>
> ### 1 Samuel 20:41
> *After the boy had gone, David got up from the south side of the stone and bowed down before Jonathan three times, with his face to the ground. Then they kissed each other and wept together—but David wept the most.*
>
> ### 2 Samuel 1:26
> *I grieve for you, Jonathan my brother;*
> *you were very dear to me.*
> *Your love for me was wonderful,*
> *more wonderful than that of women.*

I do not plan to provide an exegetical analysis of these verses and their respective passages. That would take way too long! I would, however, like to share two things regarding modern interpretation of these verses. First, we must be mindful of the

---

[20] There are other Scriptures that have been utilized in the debate about David and Jonathan's relationship, but the ones listed are the most prominent. Other considered texts are 1 Samuel 20:11, 17; 23:15-18.

large interpretive gap that exists between us and these verses. The world in which these verses were penned was much different than the world today. Consider the example of kissing as is mentioned in 1 Samuel 20:41. Some modern interpreters view this as evidence of the two men having a sexual relationship. Kissing is different between the biblical Text and our society today. In the Bible, kissing is found in many different contexts: as a common greeting, a sign of worship to a superior, and as a symbol of fellowship among believers. Compared to the other expressions of kissing in the Bible, the sexual/romantic aspect of it is in the minority. In American culture, it is rare to view adult males kissing outside of a romantic/sexual relationship, but that was not the case in biblical times. The modern interpreter must be aware of such a cultural gap so as not to misunderstand such elements as "evidence" for a sexual relationship between David and Jonathan.[21]

Painting of David and Jonathan by Dutch painter François Venant from the 1600s. Surely, they did not wear those funny hats!

---

[21] Another example would be the covenant symbolism found in 1 Samuel 18:1-4. It seems strange to us to have someone give another person the clothes he is wearing as part of an agreement, but such was the case in covenant making. People of that time would find it strange to throw rice or bird seed into the air to celebrate a marital covenant...

Second, the particular text of 2 Samuel 1:26 has proven to be difficult to understand and deserves a closer look. Read this verse again. Concerning interpretation of this text, it is the most "open" or most difficult to understand among the texts featuring David and Jonathan, and the one that has most been used to defend the interpretation of their relationship as a sexual one.[22] Looking closely, you can see the interpretive challenges present, especially with bringing words and concepts across the cultural/time gap into the present.

Here are some specific interpretive challenges from this verse:

β   In what sense was Jonathan "dear" to David? Other translations use words like pleasant or lovely. Does this necessarily connote a sexual dimension?

β   The specific grammar and how it is translated affects our modern reading. How is the Hebrew word לי to be understood? It can be translated as "to me" or "for me." Is David talking about his perspective (that how it looks *to me…*) or is he referring to Jonathan's love *for* him? Further, we can consider the specific method of contrast between Jonathan's love and the love of women. Is it contrasting different types of love, or the same love? Is it a contrast in degree (such as one is a deeper love)? Also, the objects of these loves are not mentioned specifically so we are left wondering as we analyze this verse with each occasion of love: whose love? What type of love? And who is the object of this love?[23] Don't you just love all this interpretive frenzy!?

β   How should we translate and understand the Hebrew term for "love" that is used for David and Jonathan? Just as in modern English, the term "love" does not necessarily imply romance/sexuality. There are multiple terms in the Hebrew that mean/are translated as "love" into

---

[22] Harding, *The Love of David and Jonathan,* 216.

[23] One paragraph from Harding's book gives a peek at the complexity of interpretation. He writes on page 217: "Is David in 2 Samuel 1:26 referring to the love of women in general, or to the love of specific women in his life…? Is the genitive here subjective or objective, that is, is David referring to the love women had, or might have for him, or is he referring to the love he had, or might have, or both? Is this love being compared with Jonathan's love for David, or with David's love for Jonathan, or both?"

English. Thus, modern readers may attribute things that are not implied by the text. Take into consideration the Hebrew word found in 2 Samuel 1:26. This word is אַהֲבָה/ahaba. David contrasts the love of women with that of Jonathan's—using ahaba to refer to each love. This word is found in this particular form 53 times in the Old Testament. A few of these are found in the book Song of Songs so some usages likely imply a sexual meaning. Yet, the majority of the usages of the word refer to the Lord's relationship with His covenant people, and no instance of the word refers to a sexual relationship between men.[24] Thus, the use of the word love is not sufficient evidence for any sexual relationship between the two.

Overall, it is difficult to find any textual evidence that would lead the modern reader to believe that David and Jonathan had a sexual relationship. Not only does the Text not lend itself to that interpretation, but traditional interpretation of their relationship throughout the centuries has gone against it. Let us look at some of the traditional understandings of the relationship between these two men, beginning with first Jewish interpretations.

Rabbi Naphtali Tzvi Yehudah Berlin, in his extensive commentary from the mid-1800s, writes that David and Jonathan did not have a relationship of equality. He comments that Jonathan loved David more than David loved Jonathan (elaborating on how David had a lesser capacity to love). Berlin's interpretation was their love was of the soul, not of a sexual sort.[25] Even further back in history, Rabbi Judah Loew writes in the 1500s about their relationship not being dependent upon anything. In a lengthy excerpt about love, he explains that "the love of David and Yehonatan was without any angle of an aspect that would be

---

24 Zehnder, "Observations on the Relationship," 139.
25 Naphtali Tzvi Yehuda Berlin, "Haamek Sheilah on Sheiltot d'rav Achai Gaon, Kidmat Haemek, Part III 5:7," trans. Elchanan Greenman, Sefaria, accessed April 3, 2025, https://www.sefaria.org/Haamek_Sheilah_on_Sheiltot_d'Rav_Achai_Gaon?tab=contents.

dependent upon something at all."[26] Thus, Rabbi Loew does not see a sexual relationship but a true friendship with nothing else (physical or otherwise) depending on it. Even many modern-day Jewish interpreters rebuff against such an interpretation of David and Jonathan. Rabbi Joseph Telushkin, whom I referenced previously, disagrees with viewing their relationship as sexual. In reacting to homosexual interpretations of 2 Samuel 1:26, Telushkin says that Jonathan's love was superior to women because it was "disinterested and platonic."[27] As we can see, traditional Jewish interpretations have never embraced such an interpretation of David and Jonathan's relationship.

Now let us consider some traditional Christian interpretations of their relationship. As previously explained, the idea of David and Jonathan being in a sexual relationship did not fully appear until Jeremy Bentham's suggestion in the early 19th century. Yet, early Christian understandings and descriptions of the men's relationship point away from a sexual relationship. The early Church Father Gregory Thaumaturgus provides an early Christian understanding of David and Jonathan's relationship. In a theological argument he wrote in the 3rd century, Gregory quotes 1 Samuel 18:1: "that the soul of Jonathan was knit with the soul of David (KJV)." In his very LONG yet beautiful theological argument, Gregory uses this verse as an example of the type of connection mankind has with the Lord. The lesser entity desires to be united with the greater entity, and not the other way around. Thus, man is tied up with the Divine since the Divine is so much nobler and grander.[28] In this way, Gregory understood that Jonathan, as the lesser, was

---

[26] Judah Loew, "Derekh Chayyim 5:17:7," trans. R. Francis Nataf, Sefaria, accessed April 3, 2025, https://www.sefaria.org/Derekh_Chayyim.5.17.7. Yehonatan is the Hebrew transliteration of the name we translate as Jonathan.

[27] Telushkin, *Biblical Literacy*, 211.

[28] Gregory Thaumaturgus, *Ante-Nicene Fathers: The Writings of the Fathers down to A.D. 325*, ed. Alexander Roberts and James Donaldson, vol. 6 (Peabody: Hendrickson, 1995), 28. Greg writes later on: "Nor is it, in my opinion, in the inferior subject, who is changeful and very prone to vary in purpose, and in whom singly there has been no capacity of union at first, that the power of loosing the sacred bonds of this affection rests, but rather in the nobler one, who is constant and not readily shaken, and through whom it has been possible to tie these bonds and to fasten this sacred knot." It's wordy, but that's the Gospel baby! The Lord alone can do the work.

knit together with David, the greater one, in the same way that mankind is drawn to the Divine. As the reader can see, there is no understanding of a sexual relationship, but Gregory views it as a comparison with man's relationship with the Lord.

Fast forward to John Wesley in the 18th century. John Wesley's notes on the Bible give us insight into his interpretation of the relationship of David and Jonathan. From 1 Samuel 18:4, John Welsey remarks that Jonathan loved David for "for his excellent virtues and endowments, which shone forth both in his speeches and actions; for the service he had done to God and to his people; and for the similitude of their age and qualities."[29] In another place, Wesley refers to their relationship as a true friendship.[30] Wesley viewed the two as the best of friends but without any hint of sexuality involved.

After reviewing all of these things, how should we understand the relationship between David and Jonathan? Given the late introduction in history for interpreting David and Jonathan as having a sexual relationship, the burden of proof belongs to those that would argue for the two having a sexual relationship. The Texts do not appear to support that. When homosexual activity is mentioned in the Old Testament, the Text uses the Hebrew words of יָדַע/yada or שָׁכַב/shakab. These words are never used in the context of David and Jonathan's relationship.[31] There are better ways to understand their close-knit relationship. One angle to look at their relationship is between two friends who support and care for one another without any agenda. Their loyalty and connection with each other may have been greater than that in many marriages but that doesn't imply that it was sexual.[32] Another angle to understand their relationship is through the

---

[29] John Wesley, "Wesley Center Online," The Wesley Center Online: John Wesley's Notes on the Bible, accessed June 5, 2025, https://wesley.nnu.edu/john-wesley/john-wesleys-notes-on-the-bible/.
[30] Note from 1 Sam. 20:17.
[31] Zehnder, "Observations on the Relationship," 156-157.
[32] David himself had multiple wives. Some of his marriages had political motives. Thus, thinking about a strong friendship with another person with no ulterior motives makes sense and would be valuable.

lens of ancient male bonding.[33] Sure, you can look at it alongside the other *paria amicorum*, but you can also just consider their relationship alongside other character dyads in the Bible (Paul and Barnabas, Elijah and Elisha, etc.). Two males sharing a commitment to one another does not imply anything sexual. Yes, in our modern sensibilities we wouldn't describe such a loyal friendship in the way that the Text does (perhaps we would say "bromance"), but certainly the reader need not jump to a sexual interpretation. David and Jonathan's relationship can serve as an example of an authentic and valuable friendship between two males that is emotionally rich without being sexualized.[34]

Allow me to offer some concluding thoughts on this topic. First, does it matter if David and Jonathan had a sexual relationship? In one sense, this question is not vital to the Christian faith. Our faith is in Jesus Christ, not King David. King David is a prominent figure in the Bible, but he is never said to be perfect. 1 and 2 Samuel record his sins and shortcomings. There is only one person who has truly been sinless and perfect, and it is in HIM that we place our trust. While it may not be a vital blow to the Christian faith, it still is an important issue with how we read the Bible and understand the characters within it. If such an interpretation of David and Jonathan is permissible, what's next? A search for every possible character who may have an alternative sexual orientation? Finding vampires or aliens in the Bible? A great concern of mine is how the Text is being utilized. It bothers me greatly when people find opportunities to support their own agenda because some verses contain enough vagueness or openness to get away with it.

---

[33] Anthony Heacock, "Wrongly Framed? The 'David and Jonathan Narrative' and the Writing of Biblical Homosexuality [Sic]," *The Bible and Critical Theory* 3, no. 2 (2007): 22.1-22.14, https://doi.org/10.2104/bc070022, 22.10. Heacock elaborates: "Jonathan's self-emptying of his identity into David as a hero-worshipper, and the concomitant closeness it brings, is not an issue of (homo/bi) sexuality as reflective of the gender politics of ancient male bonding. In other words, Jonathan's loyalty and subservience is less a feminine trait signifying homosexual
tendencies than a characteristic trait of the dyadic relationships inherent to ancient male bonding between heroic men, whereby there can only be one 'top dog' and, in this instance, that is David."

[34] Zehnder, "Observations on the Relationship," 174.

With that established, I do not believe that David had a sexual relationship with Jonathan. If this were true, why would the author of 1 and 2 Samuel not record it? The author does not shy away from David's terrible sin of adultery and murder in 2 Samuel chapter 11. After these events, the prophet Nathan confronts David about his sinfulness. A commonsense approach would ask why the same wouldn't occur if this were true of David and Jonathan as it violates the Mosaic Law.

The dissemination of this interpretation of David and Jonathan's relationship is a profoundly negative employment of the Humpty Dumpty Effect. This alternative reading of their relationship hints that a prominent person in Scripture held a secret sin or way of life without the Text addressing it directly. The troublesome interpretative situation is summarized well by James Harding in his book on this topic: "The way we read texts, even the very questions we ask of them, are already determined by their prior reception. In a similar vein, I am arguing that it is difficult now to read the David and Jonathan narrative other than through the lens of its nineteenth-and early twentieth-century history of reception."[35] While it may be difficult, it is not impossible to let the Text speak on its own accord. Let those who study the Text look at it with fresh eyes—seeing what it says and doing their best not to utilize their own agenda.

Print entitled "Parting of David and Jonathan." Caspar Luyken, 1712.

---

[35] Harding, *The Love of David and Jonathan*, 404.

CHAPTER 5:
THE MAGI AND THE NATIVITY SCENE

"We three kings of Orient are;
Bearing gifts we traverse afar–field and fountain,
moor and mountain-Following yonder star."
John H. Hopkins Jr., 1857, "We Three Kings."

It's a marvelous sight we are all familiar with—the Nativity Scene. Baby Jesus lying calmly in a manger with Mary and Joseph on either side of him in reverential awe. Surrounding the trio are all sorts of barnyard animals, shepherds with their canes adoring the newly born child. Then, up in the air, there is the Christmas Star and an angel of the Lord. Lastly, nearly every Nativity scene includes three royally dressed guests—the three magi. Yet, this scene, despite all of its simplistic beauty and allure, is not quite right…

Before I proceed, let me share this so that the reader does not identify me as a theological grinch: both Christmas and the Nativity scene are beautiful and wonderful. The Nativity scene is a wonderful religious image that points admirers to the ultimate message of Christmas: the Lord has come to us! Immanuel! This is the message that all need to hear. As much as Christians may lament the secularization and commercialization of the Christmas season, the Nativity scene is still prevalent, and it points people toward the reason for the season. However, I have two main beefs with the Nativity scene. First, it is too sanitized. Look at a Nativity scene and observe the people. Nearly all the characters look angelic. The only character that should look angelic is the angel. Baby Jesus, who is often presented as being much older than a newborn lying in a manger, looks calm. Some portrayals even have a halo above his head. Mary looks like she recently got a makeover instead of just enduring childbirth without any meds. Joseph looks well-rested instead of an anxious basket-case who just had to cut the umbilical cord of a child. It all seems too staged and not an accurate picture of a couple who just delivered a child in a questionable environment. My second complaint about the traditional Nativity scene is that it is not biblically accurate. Its portrayal of the characters being simultaneously present in the scene is not in line with the testimony of the Scriptures. In the New Testament, we only have two accounts about the birth of Jesus and His infancy: Matthew 1:18-2:12 and Luke 2:1-40. Besides Jesus, Mary, and Joseph, the characters are not mentioned as being all together at the same time. The shepherds and the angels are in one narrative. The magi have a narrative of their own from the Gospel of Matthew. The animals present are there because of creative liberties.[1] The characters and images of the scene are all squashed in together when the testimony from Scripture is that some of them are separate features. For more information about Scripture's portrayal of Jesus' birth and what we know about it, check out the appendix at the end of the book.

---

[1] It's often assumed there were animals present at Jesus' birth because of the presence of the manger, but the Text never specifies that. We certainly don't know what animals, if any, were present at the Nativity. We often see donkeys, sheep, and cattle present in the Nativity scene, but we cannot rule out lions, ligers, or chupacabras.

The one feature of the Nativity scene that has the most assumptions made about it is the presence of the three magi. As we have explored in other sections, the three magi have become a Humpty Dumpty for us. In this section, we will take a closer look at the magi, our interpretation of them, how this interpretation shapes our "Nativity scenes" and our general understanding of the birth of Jesus in general and specifically Matthew chapter 2.

FILLING IN THE GAPS

Imagine if I wrote an award-winning story about a character named Johnny. It's a simple and direct story. Here it goes...Johnny goes to the store one day to buy bread. At the store, a man tries to steal food from the store. Johnny stops the man. The man then goes to jail. Johnny is hailed as a hero. The end.

Pretty epic, right? Believe it or not, I wrote that by myself with no help from Chat GPT. After the release of said story, the masses love this work of literature and people start hoping and praying that they turn the story of Johnny into a movie. So, of course, "Johnny Goes to Buy Bread" becomes a movie. Now, think about this: when this short work of literature is transformed into a movie, things must be added into the story that aren't in the text. Let us briefly think of two specific examples. First, the character of Johnny. Nothing is said about his age, relationship status, ethnicity, location, etc. By choosing an actor to play Johnny, details not in the text have to be invented. Second, how does Johnny stop the person from stealing food at the store? Does he use persuasive words? Does he have a weapon? Does he recognize the thief as his long-lost brother and convince him to give up a life of crime and come home to see the family goats? Again, by moving from written text to something more (image, movie, expanded written work), details are inserted that were not present originally.[2]

Although *Johnny's Big Day*[3] is completely made up, the issue that presents itself when moving from text to something else is a true reality for all forms of literature.

---

[2] Regardless of how the rest of the movie version goes, it must end with Johnny at home eating a grilled cheese sandwich with his newly purchased bread.
[3] Working title.

This is especially true of the Bible. Whenever a story from Scripture is cast into an image or created into a video, decisions have to be made that are not in the Text. In other words, the gaps have to be filled. Filling in the gaps in a story comes very naturally for us—we often do so without realizing we are. When you read the story about Johnny, you probably visualized how the story would look like in reality (in your mind, you probably had Johnny walking or driving to the store, but actually he rode backward on a tricycle). We may unknowingly fill in the gaps in the Scriptures when we read them. Consider the book by Rev. Jesse Lyman Hurlbut, *Hurlbut's Life Of Christ For Young And Old*, published in 1915. In the preface of the book, Rev. Hurlbut wrote: "In order that this book may not lead its younger readers or listeners away from the Bible, but directly toward it, no imaginary scenes or conversations have been introduced."[4] Not trying to diss Rev. Hurlbut's book, but how is it possible that nothing is added to the Gospels when his book is almost 500 pages long?[5] That's a lot longer than all four Gospels combined! The answer to this comes from filling in the gaps. Filling in the gaps is not necessarily wrong; we just have to be mindful of our own interpretative stance and what we, as readers, bring into the interpretation. No reader is completely objective, but we can work at being better readers of the Bible, being mindful not to interject items into the Text that are not there.

---

[4] Jesse Lyman Hurlbut, *Hurlbut's Life of Christ For Young and Old* (Philadelphia, PA: The John C. Winston Company, 1915), 3.

[5] I give credit to Eric Vanden Eykel for sharing this example from his book on the magi. He will be cited later.

Filling in the gaps of Bible narratives

One of the difficult things for modern readers of the Bible is not having all the details that we would like. It is common to read a great passage of Scripture and wonder about all sorts of things that are not recorded in the Text. As I have shared, anytime we move from the actual Text of the Bible to another expression of it, gaps need to be filled in.

Suppose you want to create a painting or work of art depicting a scene from the Bible. How do you faithfully do that? Perhaps you want to write about a character from the Word of God or do a "spin-off" of a passage or person. How should that be done without distorting the meaning of the original Text?

Here are some strategies for filling in the gaps.

❖ Ask yourself these questions: What known sources are helping to fill in the gaps? Are these sources credible, or just speculation? What is influencing my interpretation of the Text? Does this gap filling contradict the portion of Scripture I am reading or another part of Scripture? Does it detract from the main point?

➢ Let us consider the magi as our practical examples. The magi are commonly portrayed as riding on camels even though their mode of transport is never specified in the Bible. To show them as being on camels is not a big deal as long as we read that back into the Text. If one makes an image of the magi traveling to see Jesus, a mode of transportation has to be chosen…camels, horses, walking, Harley-Davidson motorcycles. If the latter is chosen, it detracts from the main focus of the Text's narrative about Jesus.

❖ Be mindful of the *sitz im leben*. This is German for "Setting in Life." In other words, the context of the day.

➢ How do we understand and view the gifts to Jesus in Matthew 2. Birthday gifts? No. Gifts to honor a king? Yes.

> Make sure that the gap filling is not anachronistic. Although it would be totally rad, the magi riding on motorcycles would be in violation of the *sitz im leben* of the Ancient Near East.

❖ Keep the main thing the main thing. Christ is ultimate. Our faith, our lives, the Church—they all have Christ as our foundation. After that, we look to the canon which reveals God and His will for our lives. Other things that we may use to fill in the gaps are not inspired and are not part of the canon. Thus, readers of the Bible must be careful not to place them into the Text.

❖ As a positive example of gap filling, I would like to highlight a recent book written by Kathie Lee Gifford (yes, that's the lady from daytime television) and Brian Litfin.[6] This book explores the events surrounding the birth of Jesus with a special focus on Mary and King Herod. While the details from these events in Scripture are relatively few, gap filling is done, but it is done in a logical and faithful manner. Litfin is transparent in sharing the extracanonical sources from which he gathers ideas (some of which are mentioned in this book). I don't agree with everything in its presentation, but it remains faithful to the message of Scripture. Overall, it is a great read that doesn't violate the Bible itself.

---

[6] Gifford, Kathie Lee, and Bryan M. Litfin. *Herod & Mary: The True Story of the Tyrant King and the Mother of the Risen Savior.* Nashville, TN: W Publishing Group, an imprint of Thomas Nelson, 2024.

WHAT DO WE KNOW ABOUT THE MAGI?

The common perception of the magi (especially as depicted in the Nativity scene) contains a lot of gap-filling, and many readers are not even aware what they "know" about the magi is not in the Text. It's not an understatement to say that the magi have developed a wholly separate identity outside of the biblical Text.

Let's examine how the magi are understood today. First and foremost, the large majority of people in the western world view the number of magi as three. This was largely confirmed by the personal surveys I conducted. Nearly 50% of responses said that there were three magi. One person said 9.

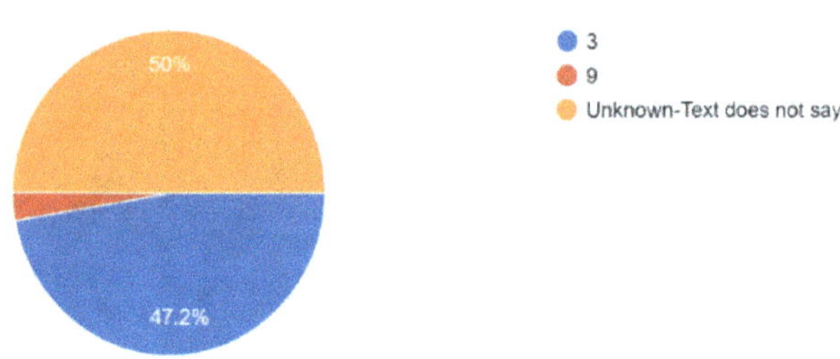

The belief that there were three magi is very popular. Just about every Nativity scene contains three magi presenting gifts to baby Jesus.[7] January 6 is the Christian holy day of Epiphany; it also frequently goes by the title Three Kings Day. The magi are often described as either wise men or kings. The names given to the three magi are Balthazar, Caspar, and Melchior.[8] Furthermore, the magi are often depicted as having different ethnicities. As we shall see, much of what we assume about the magi has no basis in the Text. The gap-filling of these mysterious men has created a new identity. Let us now turn to look in detail at the Text in Matthew chapter 2—ascertaining what we know with certainty about the magi, and exploring how our perception of them has been shaped from some translations of Matthew 2, prior interpretations of that chapter, especially early retellings of the Nativity story in the first millennium AD.

What do the Holy Scriptures tell us about the magi that came to visit Jesus? Honestly, not very much. The magi "magically" appear in Matthew 2 and by the end of the chapter they are gone forever (unlike the McRib sandwich which will perennially reappear). There is no other reference to them in the Bible. Additionally, the term "magi" is commonly misunderstood. The Greek word for magi is μάγοι/magoi; singular is μάγος/magos. While we often think of the term referring to a wise man, the term actually denotes a person who practices magic (magi-magic…surely, we see the connection!). There are only 2 other passages

---

[7] Honestly, I don't think I have seen one without three magi. What about you?

[8] There are several alternative spellings for their names.

outside of Matthew 2 where this word and its cognates are found in the New Testament. The first concerns a man named Simon in Acts 8:9-11. Simon is said to practice magic (verb form of magi) and to amaze the people with his magical abilities in a city in Samaria. Later in the chapter, Simon tries to purchase the power of the Holy Spirit from the Apostles. The second occurrence is found later in Acts 13:6-8:

> *There they met a Jewish sorcerer and false prophet named Bar-Jesus, who was an attendant of the proconsul, Sergius Paulus. The proconsul, an intelligent man, sent for Barnabas and Saul because he wanted to hear the word of God. But Elymas the sorcerer (for that is what his name means) opposed them and tried to turn the proconsul from the faith.*

In these verses, the Greek word of magos is translated as "sorcerer."[9] The history of the term prior to its usage in the New Testament shapes our perception of the magi in Matthew 2. The term "magi" appears to derive from the Old Persian word *magush.*[10] Many interpretations of the magi in Matthew convey that these men are Zoroastrian diviners from Persia (a few other places are theorized but Persia seems to be the most common). A large reason for this is because of the existence of a priestly caste of magi found in Persia and Media in the centuries before Christ. The Greek historian Herodotus, who lived and wrote in the 4th century BC, shared how these magic priests served as royal advisers in their lands; they demonstrated great knowledge in their "magic" which consisted of astrology and dream interpretation.[11] If there were no other understandings of magi at that time except for the caste of Persian magi, then we would know with certainty the

---

[9] It is interesting to note how the same word is translated differently in Acts as opposed to Matthew. Truly, even biblical translation is not always a completely objective enterprise.

[10] Titus M Kennedy, *Excavating the Evidence for Jesus: The Archaeology and History of Christ and the Gospels* (Eugene, OR: Harvest House Publishers, 2022), 41.

[11] Walter A. Elwell and Philip Wesley Comfort, eds., *Tyndale Bible Dictionary* (Wheaton, Ill: Tyndale House Publishers, 2001), 843.

background of the magi in Matthew 2. Yet not all references to magi in literature around that time was to this group of Persian magi. The term is used in three other senses beyond the Persian magi caste, containing both positive and negative associations.[12] Likewise, the Septuagint uses the word magoi for the Babylonian magicians under King Nebuchadnezzar. These magi would have been Babylonian and not Persian.[13] In the centuries prior to Christ's advent, we find that magi came to be utilized as more of a generic term for magic practitioners rather than simply a specific caste from Persia or Medes. Thus, magi came to be understood as those who practice magic, dream interpretation, or astrology.[14] Considering all of these things, we are left with a lot of openness as to the characteristics of the magoi in Matthew 2—we cannot state with certainty that they are of the Persian magi caste. We don't know with certainty about their specific abilities and powers except with the general understanding of magical abilities in the realm of performing wonders and possibly dream interpretation. Scholar Eric Vandel Eykel, who has written an entire book on the magi, points out that "there is no widespread agreement in the ancient world on who and what *magoi* were and how they should be understood."[15]

Since there was no such universal understanding of what magi were in that time period, we must confess that we have limited knowledge about the magi in Matthew chapter 2. Some readers may automatically view them as Persian priests, but that is not stated and would not have been assumed at that point in history or by Matthew's original audience.[16]

---

12 Timothy P. Hein, "The First Christian 'Magicians': Early Christian Afterlives of Matthew's Magi (Matt 2:1-12)," *The First Christian "Magicians": Early Christian Afterlives of Matthew's Magi (Matt 2:1-12)* (thesis, University of Edinburgh, 2021), 24. Negative associations such as deceivers and traitors, but positive associations such as healers or performing wondrous works.

13 For example, see Daniel 1:20, 2:2.

14 Kennedy, *Excavating the Evidence,* 41.

15 Eric Vanden Eykel, *The Magi: Who They Were, How They've Been Remembered, and Why They Still Fascinate* (Minneapolis, MN: Fortress Press, 2022), 65.

16 It is possible that the magi were Zoroastrian priests from Persia or elsewhere, but we are seeking to find what we know with a degree of certainty. That would be an assumption that's not necessary.

Let us look at the verses that feature the Magi in the Gospel of Matthew.

> *After Jesus was born in Bethlehem in Judea, during the time of King Herod, Magi from the east came to Jerusalem and asked, "Where is the one who has been born king of the Jews? We saw his star when it rose and have come to worship him."*
> (Matthew 2:1-2)

The magi make their appearance after Jesus was born. The only textual clue to their origin is that they are "from the east." Certainly, it was not a couple miles to the east outside of Jerusalem—that would have been insignificant! Yet, the east is pretty ambiguous, allowing for many speculations as to the exact origin of the magi. Some early Church fathers theorized that they arrived from Arabia as that would have been a likely place for their gifts to the Christ Child to originate from.[17] Others have suggested they are from Persia, Chaldea, or even as far east as China. Admittedly, these are theories and speculations—we honestly don't know where they originated from. Matthew's concern doesn't seem to be specifically where they came from, but on why they arrived in Jerusalem. They arrived to worship the one born King of the Jews.

When the magi arrived in Jerusalem, they did not know that the One they were looking for was born in Bethlehem. Logically, it made sense for the magi to go to Jerusalem. Jerusalem was the location of the Temple, the center for Jewish religious practice, and also where the King of the Judeans lived since the days of King David.[18] The magi asked the powers that be where the new king is. Herod was disturbed when he heard this question (I will share more on King Herod later in detail…but wouldn't you be disturbed if someone showed up asking about interviewing for *your job???*).

---

[17] Elwell and Comfort, *Tyndale Bible Dictionary*, 843. Both frankincense trees and myrrh trees grow in the Arabian peninsula.
[18] Vanden Ekyl, *The Magi*, 79-80.

After consulting with the chief priests and scribes, Herod sends the magi to Bethlehem where Jesus, the Messiah, is to be born. The remainder of the passage gets back to the actions of the magi.

> *After they had heard the king, they went on their way, and the star they had seen when it rose went ahead of them until it stopped over the place where the child was. When they saw the star, they were overjoyed. On coming to the house, they saw the child with his mother Mary, and they bowed down and worshiped him. Then they opened their treasures and presented him with gifts of gold, frankincense and myrrh. And having been warned in a dream not to go back to Herod, they returned to their country by another route.*
> (Matthew 2:9-11)

The magi depart from Jerusalem and, guided by the star, end up at the house where Jesus and Mary are. Here, the magi do what they came to do—they bow down and worship Jesus. They present him with their gifts of gold, frankincense, and myrrh. At some point shortly after, the magi were warned in a dream not to return to Herod.[19] Therefore they returned to the east and went home, making sure to avoid Herod along the way.

What do we truly know about the magi from the Text of Matthew chapter 2? Is this passage a random story about a group of guys who travel a long way to drop off some Christmas gifts and then return home? It is certainly more than that. There are a handful of significant things that we can ascertain from the Text.

---

[19] A couple interesting items to consider. First, the details about the dream. Who had the dream? One magus? All of the magi? And when did they have the dream? One would imagine that night, since Bethlehem and Jerusalem were only six miles apart. Second, how does Matthew know about the dream? Like many items in the Gospels, such as Jesus' thoughts or things unknowable by man, we have to trust in divine inspiration for such things.

The magi were Gentiles.

It is possible for magi to be Jewish (cf. Elymas the sorcerer from Acts 13:6-8). Yet, the implicit impression is that our magi from Matthew 2 are Gentiles. They come from the east-very likely outside of Judea. Furthermore, they come seeking the King of the Jews. If they were Jewish, they would have simply arrived to worship *their king*.

As Gentiles, the magi coming to visit Jesus demonstrates a key theme in the Gospel of Matthew and the entire New Testament: non-Jewish people, the Gentiles, putting their faith in Jesus. Jesus' manifestation to the Gentiles is a key facet of the Christian holiday known as Epiphany. Epiphany is 12 days after Christmas and occurs on January 6th; it is also known as Three Kings Day because of its connection with the magi. Even if we don't belong to a Christian church tradition that emphasizes Epiphany, we definitely must be grateful for the Gospel being revealed to the Gentiles.

The magi came to worship Jesus.

The Text makes it clear their aim is to worship. The Greek word used in the passage is προσκυνέω/proskuneó. While some translations may translate this word as "kneel before" or "pay homage to," "worship" is the best understanding.[20] In Matthew's Gospel, the word is only used in reference to God (God the Father or Jesus). New Testament Scholar Mark Allan Powell has studied the use of this word in Matthew's Gospel. He writes that proskuneó "describes reverence or devotion that should only be rendered to God or to one regarded as God's equivalent."[21] Tracing the use of this word through Matthew proves this theory. When Jesus is facing temptations from the devil in the wilderness, He says to him,

---

[20] The Greek word is a combination of to/toward and the verb for kissing. A literal rendition means to kiss toward someone or kissing the ground. The intent is not literal but conveys the sense of one being prostrate with a head bowed toward the ground in adoration. Thus, some translations like "bow down" are sufficient but don't fully carry the standard literary intent of worship.

[21] Mark Allan Powell, *Matthew: An Interpretation Bible Commentary* (Louisville, KY: Westminster John Knox Press, 2023), 51.

"Worship/proskuneó the Lord your God and serve him only."[22] Thus, when the magi came to worship Jesus, they were not just honoring him like any other king. In accordance with Matthew's Gospel, they were recognizing Him as a divine king.[23]

The magi brought gifts of gold, frankincense, and myrrh to Jesus.

While these gifts may seem odd to be given to a child, they weren't specifically given to honor a child but rather a king. Perhaps you have heard of a joke or seen a comic about one of the wise men bringing diapers or baby formula? The three gifts bestowed upon the Christ Child were valuable and precious. In that day, those gifts were seen as appropriate offerings to a king or deity. In 243 BC, the ruler of the Hellenistic Seleucid empire, Seleucus II Callinicus[24] offered these exact three gifts to the Greco-Roman deity of Apollo.[25]

There is uncertainty about the whether the specific gifts given by the magi carry any special symbolism in regard to Christ's identity. Some scholars (e.g. Eric Vanden Eykel) understand the significance of the gifts only because of their value.[26] In other words, these gifts were presented to Jesus as the king because they were expensive…Kings appreciate expensive gifts and probably don't want anything from the dollar store.[27] Yet, from early on in church history, the gifts have often been interpreted in an allegorical (symbolic) fashion. Here are the typical interpretations of the gifts. Gold represents Jesus' position as King. Frankincense represents Jesus' priestly role, serving as the bridge between

---

[22] Matthew 4:10

[23] In his commentary, the previously mentioned Powell notes three different instances of worship. He classifies the magi's worship as that of devotion and awe. He describes it as such: "In these cases, people worship simply because they are aware of God's majesty and presence. They are awestruck and caught up in the splendor of a divine moment, worshiping God or Jesus for who they are, not for what they have done or might do." Powell, *Matthew*, 52.

[24] What a name. His mom probably just called him "Sel" or "boy."

[25] Kennedy, *Excavating the Evidence*, 37.

[26] Vanden Eykel, *The Magi*, 101.

[27] In that era, it may have been known as the Mite Bazaar ☺

humanity and God. Myrrh represents Jesus' later crucifixion and death on the cross.[28] We find this understanding of the magi's gifts as early as 180 AD by the Christian Bishop Irenaeus of Lyons.[29] This understanding is still common today. The hymn "We Three Kings," which was quoted at the beginning of this chapter, utilizes this symbolism. It devotes a stanza to each of the three gifts, describing their significance.

It's worth asking: is such an interpretation of the gifts warranted or appropriate? Matthew's Gospel by itself does not lend itself to such an interpretation. No significant mention of gold occurs in the remainder of this Gospel outside of the parable of the Talents. There is no other mention of frankincense in the Gospel. Likewise, there is no other mention of myrrh in Matthew's Gospel. Interestingly enough, Matthew's Gospel could have made this connection but does not. When Jesus is on the cross, He is offered wine mixed with gall to drink.[30] Yet, in the Gospel of Mark, Jesus is offered wine mixed with myrrh.[31] If Matthew's Gospel were striving to make that connection, it would have been mentioned especially here with the myrrh.

All things considered, it would be out of line to assert that Matthew's Gospel by itself supports such a symbolic interpretation. The New Testament clearly demonstrates the truth about Jesus in regard to the symbolism of the three gifts: Jesus' Kingship (gold), Jesus' priestly function (frankincense), and Jesus' sacrificial

---

[28] Gold was very often connected with being a fit gift for a king. Frankincense was used in temple worship. Myrrh was used in preparation for burial as well as embalming because of its sweet smell.
William Barclay, *The Gospel of Matthew*, vol. 1 (Philadelphia: Westminster Press, 1975), 32.
[29] A. Cleveland Coxe and Irenaeus, *Ante-Nicene Fathers: The Writings of the Fathers Down to A.D. 325*, ed. Alexander Roberts and James Donaldson, vol. 1 (Peabody: Hendrickson, 1995), 423.
Irenaeus writes, " [the magi] showed, by these gifts which they offered, who it was that was worshipped; *myrrh*, because it was He who should die and be buried for the mortal human race; *gold*, because He was a King, 'of whose kingdom is no end;' and *frankincense*, because He was God, who also 'was made known in Judea,' and was 'declared to those who sought Him not.'"
[30] Matthew 27:34
[31] Mark 15:23

death (myrrh). Yet just because those things are true does not mean it is fitting to supply that intention either to the magi or to Matthew's Gospel. We can and ought to emphasize these things about Jesus, but we ought not create special meanings for the gifts if the Text does not lend itself to that.[32]

The magi were guided by a star to Jesus.

As I wrote earlier, many magi around this time period were known for their wisdom in regard to astrology or astronomy. While we cannot state with supreme certainty, it is likely that our magi in Matthew chapter 2 had special insight into this area. Our magi have witnessed a celestial phenomenon that they recognized as significant or out of the ordinary. They said they saw Jesus' star when it rose. Later in the passage, Matthew comments that the star "stops over the place where the child was." While few details are given about the magi, we do know this "star" led them to the Christ Child.

Many over the last two millennia have wondered about this star. Theories abound for what this star was. Such theories speculate comets, planetary conjunctions, or a supernova.[33] While some of these are possible options given when they occurred[34], the trouble is in finding any celestial phenomenon or object that matches what Matthew's text describes. Matthew describes the star as "rising" and then later stopping over Jesus' house. Comets and planetary conjunctions would

---

[32] Perhaps I have stepped into a murky area here with this idea. It is far too common for Christians to make "exegetical leaps" since the conclusion is true but being unfaithful to the process of getting there. We ought to strive to get the process and the conclusion right in biblical studies.

[33] Bernard Robinson, "Matthew's Nativity Stories: Historical and Theological Questions for Today's Readers," essay, in *New Perspectives on the Nativity*, ed. Jeremy Corley (New York, NY: T & T Clark International, 2009), 110–31, 121-122.

[34] Halley's Comet appeared in 12 BC, other comets have also been speculated but not verified around that time period. A planetary conjunction between Jupiter and Saturn occurred in 7 BC; Jupiter with Venus in 2 BC. There are also reported supernovae that occurred several times during this decade. If we try to find heavenly lights that could have been the star, there are many to choose from.

not seem to fit that description. Perhaps this star was actually a "sentient agent, such as angel or divinely controlled light."[35]

Much literature has been written on this query of identifying "the star of Jesus" or "the star of Bethlehem." Since we don't know the actual year of Jesus' birth or any more information beyond what Matthew has given us, people can only make educated guesses. Returning to the concern at hand, one thing we do know with certainty about the magi is that they were led by this special star to find Jesus.

The magi met with King Herod when they arrived in Jerusalem.

The Gospel Text does not reveal all the details about their interaction, but the two parties converged in some form or another (it is doubtful that Herod invited them in for tea and biscuits). We actually don't know if the magi asked their question directly to King Herod or if Herod discovered the magi asking this question around Jerusalem.[36] Herod is greatly disturbed by their inquiry and then secretly brings in the magi to find Jesus and report back to him. Insights into why King Herod reacts the way he did are given in the next section: The Wonderful King Herod. While we may not know all the details about their meeting, we do with certainty that the magi visited King Herod, with the king sending them to Bethlehem.

THE WONDERFUL KING HEROD

Matthew chapter two introduces us to King Herod. He is often referred to as "Herod the Great." What is unclear is whether history's designation of him as "great" is true or sarcastic; most would definitely favor the latter. King Herod accomplished some great things during his reign over Judea. He held the region together in "relative" peace. He also led many splendid building projects such

---

[35] Kennedy, *Excavating the Evidence,* 40. On page 39, Kennedy writes that the Greek word for "star" was used for other items beyond actual stars to include things such as planets, comets, angels, or lights. He argues thus that the "star" in Matthew chapter 2 was not so much an actual star but a heavenly light that the magi could see.
[36] Matthew two tells us that the magi came to Jerusalem asking about the one born King of the Jews. It doesn't specify whom they asked or how.

as the desert fortress in Masada, Caesarea Maritima, and a large expansion of the Temple Complex in Jerusalem. Outside of those things, however, Herod was not very well liked.

When we learn the historical background of the "not so great" King Herod, we gain a better understanding of his behavior in Matthew chapter two. Why was Herod so disturbed at the Magi's search for the one born King of the Jews? Why did he want so badly to know where this child was? And why would he commit the massacre of the infants that we read about at the end of the chapter?[37]

An investigation of King Herod's life shows that he was unhappy, power-hungry, and extremely paranoid. Herod had ten wives. Legend has it that Herod executed one of his royal servants who, upon receiving the invitation for yet another wedding, wrote, "Maybe next time." Herod wanted "yes-men" around him. He would reward those who agreed with him and would punish those who disagreed. We see this in his quest for power and control. After gaining political control over the kingdom in 37 B.C., he executed the wealthiest 45 political opponents and took their possessions. He wanted to ensure nobody would speak out against him. His pursuit of power and control gave him great paranoia.

This paranoia revealed itself in terrible ways during his lifetime. One of his early opponents was his mother-in-law, Alexandra. She belonged to the Hasmonean family, the family from which Herod overtook the throne at the beginning of his reign. Alexandra wanted one of her relatives to have the position of high priest in Judea, specifically her son Aristobulus III. Herod finally relented, giving him the position, only to turn around and have Aristobulus drowned in a pool, making it appear to be an accident. Then, Herod imprisoned his mother-in-law,

---

[37] We do not know the number of infants murdered by King Herod during this violent episode. Some Christian traditions have speculated in the thousands...one Syrian liturgy suggests 64,000. These likely have no factual foundation. Given the size of Bethlehem at this time, it was likely around 20. Regardless of the number, it's a terrible atrocity. Number 20 comes from: Raymond E. Brown, *Birth of the Messiah; a New Updated Edition - A Commentary on the Infancy Narratives in the Gospels of Matthew and Luke* (Yale University Press, 1999), 204.

Alexandra.[38] Alexandra is later executed after she tried to assert that she was queen. Herod's paranoia over the throne increases over the years until his death in 4 B.C. By that time, he had executed many family members including the aforementioned Alexandra, a wife (Mariamne I), a brother-in-law, and three sons.[39]

The man we find as the king over Judea in Matthew chapter two is paranoid that someone would usurp his position. This is intensified by the fact that Herod himself was only a half-Jew (being from Idumea, the region south of Judea). The reader can thus understand why he felt disturbed when the magi came looking for the one born King of the Jews...

Now that we have established what we know with certainty about the magi, let us consider the common notions about them that we hear today. As we have seen, the magi have developed a life of their own outside of the biblical text. Some of these things *may be true*, but there is no biblical justification for them or historical evidence. Nevertheless, many continue to think of these ideas as coming straight from the Bible itself.

The number of magi

The common belief in Western civilization is that three magi visited the Christ Child. This likely arises from the fact that the magi gave three gifts to Jesus. Eastern tradition lists their number as 12.[40] Furthermore, an early Christian pseudepigraphic text called *The Revelation of The Magi* lists their number at 12.[41] Since this text is from the 8th century AD and is not actually written by the magi themselves, its testimony in that regard does not hold much weight. The truth is

---

[38] I know some men have trouble with their mothers in law, but certainly that's not the best solution. By the way, my mother-in-law is great and I have never had a problem with her.

[39] Elwell and Comfort, *Tyndale Bible Dictionary*, 597-598.

[40] Daniel N Schowalter, "Magi," essay, in *The Oxford Guide to People & Places of the Bible Ed. by Bruce M. Metzger; Michael D. Coogan*, ed. Michael David Coogan and Bruce Manning Metzger (Oxford: Oxford Univ. Press, 2004), 187–88, 188.

[41] Vanden Eykel, *The Magi*, 133.

we do not know how many magi there were. There could have been two, 12, 20, or some other number.

*History has forgotten about Eduardo,
the fourth magi, who forgot to bring a gift for Jesus.*

Names

Along with the magi numbering three, it is also common to hear their names as Balthasar, Melchior, and Caspar (this would only be a common thought in the West as the Eastern Church tends to view the number as 12). As we have seen, the Text of Matthew 2 does not identity the number of magi nor their names. Yet, the desire to fill in the gaps remains strong! Thus, at some point early in the history of the Christian Church, names were created for these magi.[42] These names were assigned by the 6th century AD. A mosaic from the 6th century in Ravenna, Italy features the three magi with their names. Likewise, an obscure text from the same time called *Excerpta Latina Barbari* lists these names.[43] While it is wonderful to

---

[42] Larry, Curly, and Mo would have had my vote!

[43] Vanden Eykel, *The Magi*, 67-69.

know names, the simple truth is that we have no evidence for the names of the magi.

Ethnicities

A common portrayal of the magi is for them to have different ethnicities. If you take a gander at a typical Nativity Scene, or watch a movie featuring the "three magi," there's a good chance they will have different skin tones (or at least one of them is African with dark, black skin). The ethnic variety of the magi has no evidence in Scripture. Matthew's Gospel offers no comment on their physical appearance. If anything, we can rule out the magi hailing from Africa since they were from the east (Africa is southwest of Bethlehem). Yet, this hasn't stopped the development of the magi being commonly portrayed as from different regions with different skin tones. This idea of the magi being from different regions has been around as early as the 500s, with the specific portrayal of a black magus shortly after in the Medieval period.[44]

Some have seen this interpretation of the magi as a positive thing in that it represents people from all over the world coming to worship Jesus (or at least the known parts of the world at that time: Europe, Africa, and Asia).[45] While this is true in reality and is a beautiful sentiment, it simply has no biblical justification. Furthermore, the portrayal of the black magus has been used for nefarious purposes. Biblical scholar Mark Allen Powell comments that the Church created an African magus to support colonialism. As European Christian nations began to colonize Africa, the black magus was used as a biblical example of one paying proper tribute to their overlords.[46] Additionally, there existed a relationship between the artistic portrayal of a black magus and the development of the Atlantic

---

[44] Vanden Eykel, 144. The earliest idea had the magi from Persia, Arabia, and India. At some point, one of the magi's origins shifted to Africa.
[45] Vanden Eykel, 144.
[46] Powell, *Matthew*, 47. Powell writes that "Balthasar was traditionally African was not because the church wanted to be racially inclusive, but because the church wanted Africans to pay tribute to colonial overlords who brought Christ to them."

slave trade.[47] The Humpty Dumpty Effect can sometimes be seen in negative ways. While Jesus is Lord of all the nations of the earth and commissions for disciples to be made of every nation, Scripture is silent on the specific ethnicities of the magi.

Wise Men

Perhaps the most widely held notion about the magi is their designation as "wise men." This is not to suggest that the magi from Matthew 2 were not wise or intelligent (they likely were!) but why is their identity as "wise men" so common? We don't refer to every wise character in the Bible as a wise man or woman. One plausible theory is that magi in ancient times were often part of a king's advisors. If a king needed wisdom, he would call his wise men together. Magi were among the group of "wise men" that King Nebuchadnezzar called together in Daniel 2:2. Matthew doesn't tell us if our magi were part of any royal advisory committee (although they may have been. We simply don't know). The main reason the magi are commonly designated as wise men is because of the original English translations of the Bible. Most early English translations of the Bible (Wycliffe

____

47 Paul H. D. Kaplan, *The Rise of the Black Magus in Western Art* (Ann Arbor, Mich: UMI Research Press, 1985), 3. An interesting book, and probably the only one on this topic. It also has lots of pictures!

Bible from 1382, Geneva Bible from 1599, and King James Version from 1611) all refer to the magi as "wise men." Yet, these same translations of the Bible translate magus as "witch" or "sorcerer" when referring to Simon and Elymas in Acts chapters 8 and 13. As we have already seen, the same word is translated differently. Why translate it as "wise men?"

Research on this topic didn't yield any specific insights (calls to John Wycliffe and those of the Geneva Bible translation committee went unanswered). There are two things I would like to note on this dilemma. First, I theorize that the translators of those translations that used wise men felt stuck because of magus being a difficult word to properly translate into English. Translating magus into magician, sorcerer, or witch would have been problematic as witch trials were no small thing for Christianity in Europe. A Papal Bull was issued in 1484 from Pope Innocent VIII acknowledging the severe threat of witchcraft and authorizing inquisition and punishment of offenders. In short, the age of witch hunts had begun in full swing. These translators likely did not want to convey the magi who worshiped the Christ Child were witches or associated with sorcery in any way. A safer option was chosen—wise men.[48]

---

[48] Simon and Elymas from Acts were seen in a negative light, so translating them as sorcerers or magicians would not have been problematic. If anything, they would have served as negative examples for believers to notice.

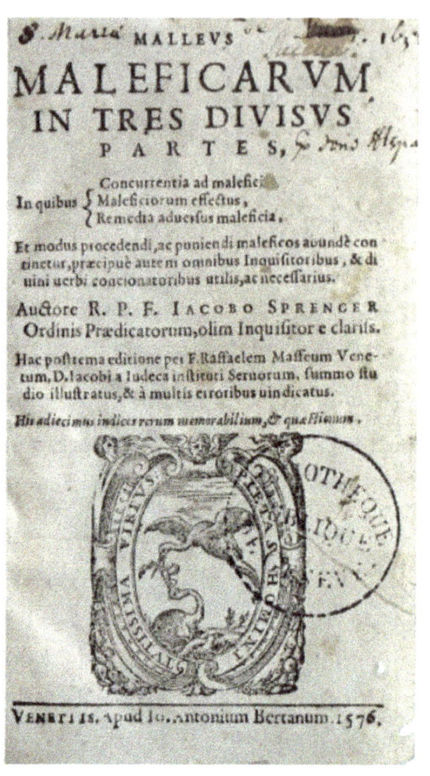

*Front page of Hammer of Witches, a treatise on witchcraft
and how to properly prosecute witches. A popular book in the
16th and 17th centuries for dealing with witchcraft.*

Second, the idea of the magi of Matthew 2 being wise men had already been around a long time before these translations were created. Chrysostom, writing in the late 4th century AD, says of the passage from Matthew 2: "A star appeared in the heavens, calling the wise men from on high."[49] As the reader can see, it was an early title and/or description of the magi. Regardless of how it originated, the concept of the magi as wise men has been around a long time and continues to shape our perception of them.

---

[49] Manlio Simonetti and Thomas C. Oden, eds., *Ancient Christian Commentary on Scripture: New Testament. 1A, Matthew 1-13* (Downers Grove, Ill: InterVarsity Press, 2001), 22.

Kings

Another common perception about the magi is that they are kings. The classic Christian hymn follows this idea in its title, "We Three Kings." In my mind, I can understand how the magi came to be described as "wise men" but it's a great leap to reckon them as kings. There is no evidence in the Text for such an interpretation.[50] As we have seen, some magi in the past served as royal advisors but they were never kings themselves.

Similar to the wise men tradition, the tradition of reading the magi as kings has existed for a long time. A gloss of the Vulgate, which was the standard Bible commentary for the Middle Ages,[51] states the magi were either kings or princes.[52] The idea had indeed been around earlier, even if it was not as widely known or believed. The French Bishop and theologian Caesarius of Arles refers to the magi as kings in a sermon in the early part of the 500s.[53] Furthermore, there are multiple references to the magi as kings of Eastern Kingdoms in the Syriac text called *The Cave of Treasures* (one of the 12 magi listed is the king of Persia who was known as the "king of kings." It is interesting how this text has this "super king" bowing down to the Christ Child).[54] Thus, we find the concept of the magi as royalty existed in the sixth century AD and widely known by the time of the Middle Ages. With no specific evidence in the Text, how did this idea come about?

---

[50] Centuries ago, both John Calvin and Martin Luther rejected this idea about the magi. Powell, *Matthew*, 47.

[51] The word "gloss" stems from Greek and Latin for "language" or "tongue." This gloss was a form of notes or explanation for difficult to understand words or phrases in the Bible. Francis Gigot, "Scriptural Glosses," Catholic Encyclopedia, accessed November 5, 2025, https://www.newadvent.org/cathen/06586a.htm#section5.

[52] Thomas Aquinas, *Catena Aurea: Commentary on the Four Gospels*, trans. John Henry Newman, vol. 1 (London: J.G.F. and J. Rivington, 1841).

[53] Mark Allan Powell, "The Magi as Kings: An Adventure in Reader-Response Criticism.," *The Catholic Biblical Quarterly* 62, no. 3 (2000): 459–80, 459.

[54] E. A. Wallis Budge, *The Book of the Cave of Treasures: A History of the Patriarchs and the Kings, Their Successors, from the Creation to the Crucifixion of Christ, Translated from the Syriac Text of the British Museum Ms. Add. 25875* (London: Religious Tract Society, 1927), 208-210.

There are two specific persons from the early centuries of the Christian Church that helped push this narrative along. First, about a century after the composition of Matthew's Gospel, Tertullian writes that the magi were "almost kings." Out of context, it is strange to think that Tertullian would make such a statement. Yet, in an argument for Christian pacificism, Tertullian claims that the magi were allegorical symbols for Old Testament kings. Powell comments on Tertullian's argument: "Notably, they are symbols of hostile kings from the past who were conquered by Christ rather than images of pious or present kings who worship him."[55] Tertullian didn't regard the magi as kings since kingly rulers do not worship Christ (Roman emperors at that time very much did not worship Christ), but he regarded them as "almost kings." This is a step toward fully identifying them as kings.

The second person that greatly pushed this narrative along is Augustine of Hippo (Hippo is a location in present-day Algeria…no connection to the animal). In a collection of Epiphany sermons delivered in the city of Hippo, he contrasts King Herod with the magi. In essence, it's a good king versus a bad king contrast. Here is what Augustine says:

King Herod, you see, was afraid, when the Magi told him about the child they were still looking for, having learned of his birth from the evidence of the heavens. How dread must be his judgment seat, when his infant's cradle could so terrify the pride of kings! How much more prudently do kings nowadays, not seek like Herod to kill, but rather delight like the Magi to worship him… Let kings now have a pious and filial fear of him, seated at the right hand of his Father.[56]

In these Epiphany sermons, Augustine views the magi as symbols for proper kings—bowing down and worshiping Christ. An examination of these sermons shows that Augustine never viewed them as literal or historical kings, but he used them as symbols to convey a point: righteous kings follow Christ and present

---

[55] Powell, *The Magi as Kings*, 474. Please note that the Tertullian's argument is long and convoluted and I am sharing in summary.

[56] Augustine, *Sermons on the Liturgical Seasons: (184-229Z)*, ed. John E. Rotelle, trans. Edmund Hill, vol. 6 (Brooklyn, N.Y: New City Press, 1993), 82-83.

treasures to Him.[57] Regardless of his intent, Augustine's treatment of the magi coupled with Tertullian's classification as "almost kings" allowed Christians in the near future to view them as literal kings. It wasn't long after that people began to read Old Testament verses as prophecies fulfilled by the "kings" of Matthew 2.

Isaiah 60:3: "Nations will come to your light, and kings to the brightness of your dawn."

Psalm 72:10-11: "May the kings of Tarshish and of distant shores bring tribute to him.
May the kings of Sheba and Seba present him gifts. May all kings bow down to him and all nations serve him."

Ultimately, we must get rid of this notion of the magi as kings. In Matthew's Gospel, it is Jesus who is the rightful king. If anything, the magi are to be seen as servants and representatives of the Gentiles coming to faith.

Magi at the stable or house

The last common perception I would like to address is the magi worshiping the Christ Child lying in the manger in the stable. Getting a detailed chronology of Jesus' infancy is tricky and nearly impossible with the data we have from the canon (I address this in detail in Appendix 1 of the book). As much as we would love to have the magi seeing Jesus in the manger (perhaps in a stable?), the Text does not give us a definitive answer to this.

---

[57] Powell, *Matthew*, 47. It's worth noting to the reader that the eras of Tertullian and Augustine were drastically different. Tertullian lived 160-240 AD which was a time when Christians were heavily persecuted. After the emperor Constantine was converted, the newly Christian emperor issued the Edict of Milan which legalized Christianity in the empire. Thus, we can see why Tertullian would say "The blood of the martyrs is the seed of the Church," but Augustine would view the magi as symbolic righteous kings.

A couple of things to note. Neither Matthew nor Luke give us a picture of Jesus with animals (that's filled in by the reader's imagination). Luke tells us Jesus was laid in a manger. Concerning the magi, Matthew 2:11 says they approached Jesus at a house. The Greek word for house is οἶκος/oikos and refers to a house, home, or dwelling. It's ambiguous enough for us to not settle the matter in what type of building structure Jesus was in. Common theories about Jesus' birthplace range from a stable to a regular house to a cave. Yet, the late biblical scholar William Barclay offers us an insight that shows that all three of these could be a possibility. He wrote: "The houses in Bethlehem are built on the slope of the limestone ridge; and it is very common for them to have a cave-like stable hollowed out in the limestone rock below the house itself; and very likely it was in such a cave-stable that Jesus was born."[58] In the end, we don't know the structure of Jesus' dwelling at this point so the Nativity scene portrayal of the magi at a stable is speculative.[59]

Now that we have examined in detail common notions about the magi, let us take a brief survey of literary texts that have shaped our perception of the magi as well as the Nativity scene/Christmas story. The ideas found in these various non-canonical sources have aided to promulgate various ideas about the magi that are

---

[58] Barclay, *Matthew*, 24.
[59] Chronology and locations are considered in Appendix 1.

not in the Text of the Bible. Some of the writings include interesting tidbits that I will share with the reader. If anything, you can use these random ideas to impress your friends or win at Pseudepigrapha Jeopardy.

EARLY LITERARY INFLUENCES ON THE NATIVITY

Protoevangelium of James

This manuscript is an "infancy gospel" or "protoevangelium" since it addresses the early years of Jesus before His public ministry. It was written in the late 100s A.D. and claims to be by written by James, the brother of Jesus (obviously, this is not possible since Jesus' brother would not have been alive then).[60] The original author (not James, but someone else) takes great liberties to fill in the gaps of the time around Jesus' birth. Here are some examples:

Joseph is a widower and already has sons before marrying Mary.

A conference is held at the Temple to find a husband for Mary who is only 16 years old.[61] Joseph is designated to marry the young lady, despite his initial opposition.

Mary travels on a donkey on their voyage to Bethlehem. Her labor progresses as the couple near Bethlehem. From there, they go to a cave for Jesus to be born.

Joseph leaves Mary in the cave with his sons and he goes to find a midwife to assist with the birth.[62]

At Jesus' birth, a blinding light filled the cave so that those within could not see.[63]

---

[60] Vanden Eykel, *The Magi*, 113.

[61] The age of Mary actually varies in the manuscript between 12 and 17.

[62] As a father of three, I say Joseph made a good call in going to find a midwife...although it may have been awkward for his sons to be left alone with a woman in labor..

[63] Willis Barnstone, *The Other Bible: Jewish Pseudepigrapha, Christian Apocrypha, Gnostic Scriptures, Kabbalah, Dead Sea Scrolls* (San Francisco etc.: HarperSanFrancisco, 1984), 385-392.

The Protoevangelium of James is the earliest apocryphal story about the magi.[64] Thus, we find a few changes from Matthew's Gospel regarding the magi. In this story, the magi never go to Jerusalem; they only go to Bethlehem inquiring about the new king. Herod summons the magi and they explain to him about the star, but this text never says they go to Jerusalem. As well, the magi go to the Christ Child in the cave where He was just born. The star goes into the cave and rests above Jesus' head.

From this early apocryphal retelling of Jesus' birth, we see a few items that have pervaded the Christmas story but are not in the Bible itself: Mary on a donkey, Mary's age, and Jesus' birth in a cave.

The Gospel of Pseudo-Matthew

This literature also goes by the other titles of *The Infancy Gospel of Pseudo-Matthew* or *The Book about the Origin of the Blessed Mary and the Childhood of the Savior*. It is probably best to stick with the shortest title here! It was written in Latin in the 6th or 7th century AD.[65] Thus, it is many years older than Matthew's actual Gospel and the *Protoevangelium of James*. This book contains a lot of the same ideas presented by the prior infancy Gospel. It supports the idea that Mary rode upon a donkey (the text says beast, but we can probably assume it was a donkey or a camel. It is highly unlikely it was the chupacabra). Likewise, Mary goes into a cave to give birth to Jesus, but it's emphasized that it's an underground cave that becomes filled with light when Mary enters.[66] This text also says that Mary experienced no pain and there was no blood shed when Jesus was born; it also emphasizes her continual virginity.[67] *The Gospel of Pseudo-Matthew* also presents us with a common feature of many Nativity scenes—the animals adoring Jesus. It

---

[64] Vanden Eykel, *The Magi*, 114.

[65] James Keith Elliott, *A Synopsis of the Apocryphal Nativity and Infancy Narratives* (Leiden: Brill, 2016), xiv.

[66] Elliot, 61, 64.

[67] Elliot, 77. Much to the jealousy of every mother on earth...

states that after Mary emerged out of the cave with the Child, they settled in a stable where Jesus was adored by an ox and a donkey.[68]

We find new insights in this text regarding the magi. The text says that the magi saw the star at the time when Jesus was born, and they arrive two years later to visit Him (they either got lost or stopped at every Buc-ee's along the way).[69] When the magi finally arrive to visit Jesus, they present their gifts of gold, frankincense, and myrrh, but these are specifically given to Mary and Joseph. But they didn't forget little Jesus—each of the magi give the Infant King a gold coin.[70] *The Gospel of Pseudo-Matthew* also includes the magi returning a second time to adore the Christ Child after they were warned to not return to Herod (they just wanted another selfie with the little King!).[71]

---

[68] Elliot, 88-89.

[69] This also supports the theory that Jesus was two years old when the magi visited. Again, we don't know with certainty when they visited but some theories are based on Herod's massacre of the innocents two and under.

[70] Vanden Eykel, *Magi,* 120-123.

[71] Elliot, *Synopsis of the Apocryphal Nativity,* 100.

While there are many credible details about the text of *The Gospel of Pseudo-Matthew*, some of the narrative's stories demonstrate its apocryphal and legendary nature. Consider the scene when Mary, Joseph, Jesus and a few others find a cave to rest in only to discover the cave was full of dragons! Of course, there was no need to fear with the infant Jesus present. The young Child stands up, and the dragons stop to worship Him, causing no danger for the family. Later, when the family was traveling, Mary was hungry but could not reach the fruit from a nearby palm tree. The infant Jesus spoke to the tree causing it to bend down to share its fruit with Mary. Also interesting is what happens when the family flees to Egypt. Jesus and Mary enter an Egyptian temple full of idols. Upon entering, the idols throw themselves down and shake before the Incarnation of the Lord.[72] These and many other interesting stories are included in *The Gospel of Pseudo-Matthew*.

Arabic Infancy Gospel

This infancy Gospel, which borrows stories from *The Infancy Gospel of Thomas* and *The Protoevangelium of James*, was likely crafted in the 6th century AD. Because of its translation into Arabic, this work was likely used to help compose the Quran by Mohammed.[73] The *Arabic Infancy Gospel* does contain some fanciful stories such as when Jesus turned some children into goats. There are only a couple of noteworthy items regarding Jesus' birth and the magi that are not found in the other books we have looked at. The first is the account of a miraculous healing by the newly born Jesus. An elderly lady is suffering from palsy, and she is healed when she places her hand upon the Baby.[74] Later, the magi visit Jesus and Mary and present their typical gifts to the Holy Child. Since Mary doesn't have much to give, she gives the magi one of the swaddling bands used to wrap up her Child.[75] Afterward visiting, the star that guided the magi to Jesus took the form of an angel and guided them back to their home country. Upon their return, all the kings and leaders of their home country greet the magi and inquire about their journey. The magi show them the swaddling band. It immediately becomes an object of

---

[72] Barnstone, *The Other Bible*, 396-397.
[73] Barnstone, 407.
[74] Elliott, *Synopsis of the Apocryphal Nativity*, 79.
[75] Worst gift exchange ever!

worship! A celebration is held, a fire is created, and the band is thrown into the fire. After the fire dies, the swaddling band is discovered to be perfect as if it had not even touched a flame. The band is then deposited into their sacred treasury as a religious relic.[76] This literary work holds many new stories that are not found in the New Testament.

The Armenian Gospel of the Infancy

This infancy Gospel likely derives from the late 6th century and contains a lot of "new" accounts of Jesus' birth and the magi. Since a modern English translation of this literature nears 150 pages in length, I will only share a few items. This story of Jesus' birth includes a brand-new character! Joseph leaves the cave with Mary in labor and finds a woman who claims to be a Hebrew midwife. Plot Twist! The midwife is Eve! She declares, "I am Eve, the foremother of all, and I have come to behold with my own eyes the redemption that is wrought on my behalf."[77] As much as there is a symbolic connection with Mary and Eve, Eve never makes a literal appearance in the New Testament.

Much detailed information is offered by this document about the magi. Here are some of the key items:

The magi numbered three, and their names are Melkon, Gaspar, and Baltasar. The text says that they are kings and brothers.

The magi took armies of thousands with them to Jerusalem; the journey took them nine months.

The magi reveal that they have a secret document that was given to Adam's son, Seth. It was sealed by the hand of God and passed along in history and was kept by the ancestors of the magi. The secret document is opened and read when they visit Jesus—it is a prophecy about Jesus being God Incarnate.

---

[76] Elliott, *Synopsis of the Apocryphal Nativity*, 100-101.

[77] Abraham Terian, trans., *The Armenian Gospel of the Infancy: With Three Early Versions of the Protoevangelium of James* (Oxford: Oxford University Press, 2008), 44.

King Herod attempts to arrest the magi but the building where they are talking begins to shake. Herod and the magi escape but 72 people perish.

The magi spend three days at the cave where Jesus was born.[78]

Like many of the other infancy Gospels, this document reinforces early traditions about magi while at the same time supplying a lot of unfounded and non-canonicals details.

Revelation of the Magi

Unlike the prior works I have shared, this document focuses on the magi instead of Jesus. It goes into great detail about their background and who they are. Coming from the fictional land of "Shir," the magi are said to be a group of 12 kings or "sons of kings." Like the *Armenian Gospel of the Infancy*, they carry a secret document that goes all the way back to Seth. This secret document shares how a star will arrive one day which will lead the magi to the One born as God. The star in *Revelation of the Magi* is quite a magic star. It does more than just lead the magi to Jesus—it guides the magi safely by stopping snakes, leveling mountains, and preparing campsites. We learn that the star was present in the Garden of Eden and now leads them to Jesus.[79]

But wait for the big plot twist…the star is actually Jesus Himself! Not sure how that can be since the star goes in the cave where the baby Jesus is (there are serious theological issues with this). Afterward, the star-child (I don't know what else to call it or him…) guides the magi back to their homeland. *Revelation of the Magi* is a late document, dating to the 8th century. It greatly adds from the account that we have in Matthew chapter 2 and builds on other developed traditions about the magi.

---

[78] Terian, 48-59.
[79] Vanden Eykel, *The Magi,* 133-137.

Cave of Treasures

Cave of Treasures is a retelling of biblical history in the Syrian language. This differs from the other works in that it doesn't focus on the events surrounding the birth of Christ but consists of all of biblical history. This book stems from no later than the 6th century.[80] The title refers to a cave that is mentioned multiple times in the book. According to this biblical retelling, when Adam and Eve were expelled from the Garden of Eden, they lived in a cave for a period of time. God's angels brought precious substances into the cave—gold, frankincense, and myrrh. These were left in the cave after Adam and Eve departed.[81] Much later in history, the magi[82] gather these gifts from the cave of treasures and bring them to baby Jesus.

There are two noteworthy concepts concerning the magi found in this text. First, this text employs the symbolism of the three gifts as described earlier. It says, "the gold was for a king, the myrrh for a physician, and the frankincense for a priest, for the Magi knew Who He was, and that He was a king, and a physician, and a priest."[83] Second, the magi in this book give an additional gift to baby Jesus: thirty pieces of silver. It claims that this silver came initially from Terah, the father of Abraham. It passed down in history until the magi had it in their possession and they gave it to Jesus. Jesus gave it to the Temple treasury. Then, the same silver was given to Judas Iscariot for betraying Jesus.[84]

---

[80] Budge, *The Book of the Cave of Treasures*, xi.
[81] Budge, 17-19.
[82] This book shares two traditions of the magi—one in which there are three magi and one which there are 12. Their names are also given.
[83] Budge, 208.
[84] Budge, 212-213.

Hymns on the Nativity

Ephrem the Syrian was a Christian theologian from the 4th century, and he loved writing hymns. He composed quite a lot of hymns in his lifetime; we have at least 400 hymns that have survived to the present day.[85] A collection of his hymns focuses on the Nativity of Jesus. In these hymns the magi from Matthew 2 are mentioned. I have decided to share a few insights from these hymns because they provide an alternative viewpoint on the magi. While the majority of other texts we have referenced, including Matthew chapter 2, tend to view the magi in a completely/mostly positive light, Ephrem gives them a mostly negative portrayal. At one point they are described as "dark ones" and at another point, they are accounted as among the traitors. In one hymn, Ephrem refers to them as blind. The hymn describes it as such:

---

[85] Vanden Eykel, *The Magi*, 160.

<blockquote>
The Morning Star cast its bright beams among the darknesses, and led them [the magi] as blind men.[86]
</blockquote>

The magi are also cast as pagans worshiping other things such as fire. Upon their conversion by meeting Jesus, they gave up worshiping fire in order to know the true Fire.

<blockquote>
Fire commended Your Birth, which drew away worship from it.— The magi used to worship it: they who have worshipped before You.— They left it and worshipped its Lord; they exchanged fire for the Fire.[87]
</blockquote>

The hymns by Ephrem also say that two of the gifts presented to Christ, the gold and the incense, were connected with their former way of life: gold from dead idols and incense in worship of demons.[88] Although the magi are described negatively, their final state is good as they are converted and worship Christ. They reject a life of idolatry and shame and worship the True God in Jesus Christ. One of the lines from Hymn 14 summarizes the magi's conversion and offers encouragement to us:

<blockquote>
The Magi also sought Him, and in the manger when they found Him — instead of scrutiny worship, they offered Him in silence;— for empty strivings, oblations gave they Him.— Seek too the Firstborn, and if you find Him in the height — instead of troubled questionings, open your treasures before Him — and offer Him your works.[89]
</blockquote>

---

86 J B Morris and Edward Johnston, trans., "Hymns on the Nativity," Church Fathers: Hymns on the Nativity (Ephraim), 2023, https://www.newadvent.org/fathers/3703.htm.
87 Morris and Johnston, "Hymns on the Nativity."
88 Vanden Eykel, *The Magi*, 162-163.
89 Morris and Johnston, "Hymns on the Nativity."

Just as the magi had to leave the Christ Child and return to their own country, so I must finish this section and move on to the final chapter of this book. The magi are intriguing to us. Likely, the lack of information about them spurs on our fascination. Although a lot of the popular ideas about the magi are not actually found in Matthew chapter 2, these characters still serve as great examples for us in the faith—they sought Jesus and worshiped Him, they foreshadowed the Gentiles believing in Jesus for salvation, and they demonstrated great courage by not returning to Herod.

OBJECTS THAT AREN'T ACTUALLY THERE!

There are some mystery objects and creatures that pop up from time to time in retellings of famous Bible stories. As much as we normally think of them, they aren't in the Text.

The mysterious murder weapon: Cain's rock (Genesis 4:8-11)

The whale that swallowed Jonah. It was called "a great fish."

Saul's donkey or horse (Acts 9:3-4)

Mary's donkey as she travels to Bethlehem (Luke 2:1-7)

The camels of the magi (Matthew 2:1-12)

CHAPTER 6: THE RAPTURE

•

> *"I will see you all in class on Monday morning,*
> *unless the Lord returns.*
> *If that happens, Dr. Lewis will be teaching."*
> Dr. Brown, Church History Professor

While everyone at the party played games and talked, I sat nervously under the plastic table. It was the evening of Christmas Day, 1999. My extended family was all gathered together in a local community building for our annual Christmas party. As the party drew to a close late in the evening, I was no longer interested in playing games with my cousins or eating snacks. I knew it was about to happen.

We would soon vanish.

All of us.

Well, probably all of us…at least those who believed.

The rapture.

Not knowing enough Scripture verses to ease my anxiety (such as the one about nobody knowing the day or hour of Christ's return), I was fully convinced that this would be the day. After all, it was Christmas in the last year of the millennium.[1] If Jesus was going to come and whisk His people away from the

---

[1] Unless you consider the last year of the millennium to be 2000 since there is no year 0. Of course, that debate wasn't in my mind…I was more concerned with Pokémon and my own prophetic guesses.

earth, tonight would be the night. So, I sat under table—worried, afraid, uncertain.

As you can guess, that never happened. Neither did my follow-up prediction of New Year's Eve less than a week later. Predictions about the return of Christ or the rapture have been occurring since the early years of the Church. Just as I was convinced that Christ would return at the end of 1999, many were filled with apocalyptic conviction for the year 1000. When the year 1000 didn't yield any grand results, many thought 1033 (a millennium after Christ's death and resurrection) would bring about the return of Christ. Again, when nothing special happened, people turned their attention to 1065. In that year, Good Friday fell on the same day as Day of Annunciation.[2] Many devout believers traveled to Jerusalem in anticipation of the Lord's return.[3]

Such grandiose predictions have been occurring all the way until the present. In recent years, we still continue to hear about various end-time predictions. NASA Engineer Edgar Whisenhunt published a book entitled *88 Reasons Why the Rapture Will Be In 1988*. He later corrected himself a few times since he messed up his calculations.[4] A host of people predicted a new age or the Lord's return at the end of 1999 or at the beginning of 2000 (see I wasn't the only one!). A famous radio preacher named Harold Camping made several end-time predictions between 1994 and 2011. I remember hearing him on the radio and thinking to myself: "What sort of a crackpot Bible teacher is that!? There are thousands of people listening and being led astray!" Even this past year, a large social media following believed that the rapture would occur in September 2025.[5] People used to have to

---

[2] The Day of Annunciation celebrates the Angel Gabriel's announcement to Mary that she would conceive and give birth to Jesus. It falls on March 25—9 months from Christmas.

[3] Stanley J. Grenz, *The Millennial Maze: Sorting Out Evangelical Options* (Downers Grove, Ill: InterVarsity Press, 1992), 14.

[4] This is a very common thing when apocalyptic predictions don't come true. They recalculate and set a new date.

[5] #RaptureTok

write a book about their end-times prediction in order to gain publicity. Now, people take the lazy approach to apocalyptic mayhem by just posting about it!

A highly prominent aspect of such end-time predictions is the rapture. The popular view of the rapture is Christians instantly vanishing from the earth (or ascending up into the sky and taken away by Jesus) while the wicked remain on the earth for the final tribulation. Yet, belief in the rapture is not universally held in the Christian Church. Far from it! As I have argued in the previous chapters, popularly held interpretations of various Bible passages and end-time predictions have continued to mold our ongoing belief on what is to come. Just as many view Humpty Dumpty as an egg because they have commonly seen it portrayed as one, so too many view the rapture as an established part of the future to come because they have been surrounded by this interpretation.

Belief in the rapture has grown in popularity over the last century, especially toward the end of the 20th century. Its presence in popular culture has aided in its development. The reader has likely encountered this. The *Left Behind* book and movie series has made a huge impact on the public's perception of biblical prophecy and what is to come.[6] A famous predecessor is the 1973 movie *A Thief in the Night* in which millions of people are raptured, and the United Nations takes over and forces people to receive the mark of the beast. Also, many television shows have broadcasted the upcoming rapture and relevant biblical prophecy over the years. Dr. Jack Van Impe hosted a television series where he talked about Bible prophecy and the rapture from 1986 until his passing in 2020.[7] In a famous song from 1969, "I Wish We'd All Been Ready," Larry Norman espouses the doctrine of the rapture and shares ideas on people disappearing from the world in the blink of an eye. The refrain of the song says: "There's no time to change your mind. The Son has come and you've been left behind." I am likely not sharing anything brand-new. The majority of people know about the rapture or at least have heard of it.

---

[6] It is "only" a 12-book series. Your obligation now is just to finish this book. ☺

[7] The show was called *Dr. Jack Van Impe Presents* and was co-hosted with his wife Dr. Rexella Van Impe.

The survey conducted for this book reveals a belief in the rapture by some people. I asked people the open-ended question: What events will happen at the return of Jesus Christ? A quarter of responses had a specific mention of rapture. I imagine that if I asked specifically about the rapture, I would have received a greater response in the affirmative.[8] A couple of responses from the survey were intriguing. One person said, "sunshine and happiness." My favorite response was when someone answered, "the raptor."[9]

What events will happen at the return of Jesus Christ?
36 responses

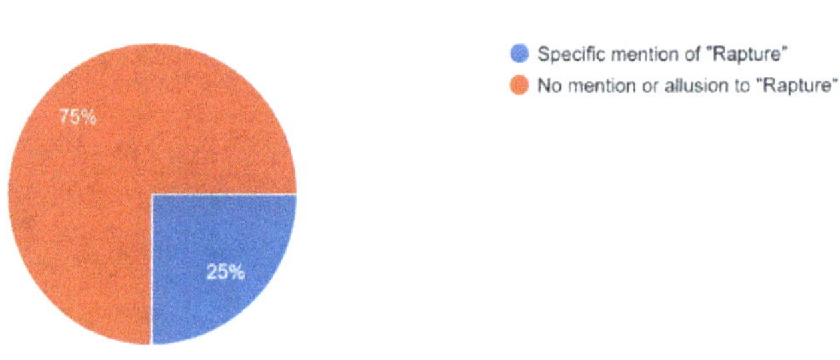

---

[8] Again, I avoided leading questions in my survey. If my toddler son can pick up on leading questions, then I assume most adults can too.

[9] Can we rule out that Jesus will return riding on a raptor?

In this final chapter of this book, I shall examine the doctrine of the rapture in biblical interpretation. Specifically, I will explain how popular cultural expressions as well as prior interpretations affect our current interpretation of biblical passages about Jesus' return. We will start with gaining a background on end-times theology. Then, we will look at the prominent views regarding end-times theology which will help us see how the rapture fits into the bigger picture. There is something worth noting before proceeding. For the sake of transparency, I do not believe in the "so-called rapture."[10] I used to believe in the rapture when I was younger. A greater understanding of the Bible and theology have led me to view the end-times in a slightly different manner. Of course, I believe in the return of Christ, the resurrection of the dead, and the Final Judgment. I just do not believe a literal "vanishing of the saints" will occur. While I may argue against the rapture in this section, my primary aim is not to have the reader abandon their belief in it. My ultimate goal is to help the reader gain knowledge in this area of theology and biblical studies as well as seeing how our prior interpretations affect our approach to the Text. On the specific matter of the rapture, we can agree to disagree.

ESCHATOLOGY AND RAPTURE

Whenever people talk about the end of the world, the rapture, or the return of Jesus, they are talking about eschatology. The word "eschatology" derives from the Greek word ἔσχατος/escatos, which means end or last. Thus, eschatology is the study of last things. Rather than it being an insignificant branch of theology, eschatology is very important and concerns the destiny of mankind. Eschatology is like peanut butter in the hands of a toddler—it gets on everything. It influences other branches of our theology, while our beliefs about God and the world influence our eschatology. It is all interconnected.[11]

Because eschatology is significant to the church, it can also be divisive. While some of the items we have examined in this book are less consequential to church unity,

---

[10] I say "so called" because the word rapture is used differently. Depending on the speaker/writing, it may have different connotations. Later, we shall arrive at a working definition of the term.

[11] Wait a moment...I need to go clean peanut butter off the fridge again.

doctrine, or morality, eschatology in general and the rapture in particular have led to arguments and even division in the church. In other words, people feel more strongly about end-times theories than the number of magi. This isn't inherently a bad thing. We ought to be concerned with the return of Jesus and what that means for our lives. In fact, eschatology **should and does** affect our present-day actions and attitude. This is true for mainstream eschatological views as well as radical stances. We hear more about the radical responses than the mainstream ones though. Consider the Branch Davidians who held strange interpretations of Revelation 5, viewing their leader as the lamb of God in that passage who must loose the seven seals. The leader of this religious sect, Vernon Howell, died along with dozens of others when their compound was sieged by the government and the building caught on fire.[12] An unchecked and wild interpretation of the Bible led to a radical interpretation which in the end resulted in the death of many people. This is but one recent example of a religious group with a radical eschatology that harmed or killed people. Sadly, history has more. Also worth mentioning are the other not as tragic examples of eschatology influencing the present. In the recent past, many have believed various end-time predictions with enough confidence to sell homes, quit jobs, and prepare for the imminent return of Jesus.[13] Getting eschatology right is very important, but getting it wrong can lead to heartache and ruin.

---

[12] It is unknown whether the fires that burned down the building were started intentionally by the Branch Davidians or if they happened accidentally as a result of the siege of the compound in Waco, Texas.

[13] Rick Paulas, "What Happened to Doomsday Prophet Harold Camping after the World Didn't End?," Vice, July 29, 2024, https://www.vice.com/en/article/life-after-doomsday-456/. One particular thing mentioned in the article is that a man donated $150,000 to the cause. It is reported that the company run by Camping spent $100 million in 2011 reporting the upcoming end of the world.

Top Divisive Church Issues

1. Christological Doctrine (e.g. Arianism)

2. Filioque Controversy

3. Women in Ordained Ministry

4. The Reformation

5. Eschatology

5. Slavery

...

351. The number of Magi

352. Did Jordan push off at the end of Game 6 in the 1998 NBA Finals?

One final thing worth noting about eschatology: it is influenced by the culture and context around us. Ideally, we would prefer to think that all of our theology is pure and objective. The hopeful image of theology development is of a person reading the Bible and gathering what is taught there without any interference. Yet, our theology, our interpretation of the Bible, nay, everything we learn is conditioned by our cultural/societal context. We live in culture as a fish swims in water.[14] There is no escape from it. Our views on eschatology are shaped by how we generally interpret the Bible as well as the *zeitgeist*[15] of the day. The general attitude of an era can lead to eschatological views reflective of that attitude. Such an idea can be seen in the history of the major viewpoints of eschatology, to which we now turn.

---

[14] Don't interpret culture as a secular spirit or antithetical to Christianity. By culture, I mean our entire context in place and time which shapes how we think, talk, act, get to work, eat...pretty much everything.

[15] German word meaning "spirit of the age." It refers to the mood or general outlook in a period of time. Just be glad I'm using that word as opposed to another German word: *Weltanschauung*. Fifty points if you know what it is without searching it online.

MAJOR POSITIONS IN CHRISTIAN ESCHATOLOGY

Eschatology addresses a lot of important questions about life, the future, Heaven, Hell, the cosmos, and God Himself. Since eschatology is chock full of ideas and interpretations, proper classification of the viewpoints is difficult. Nevertheless, major positions on Christian eschatology are usually organized into four categories. These categories revolve around the interpretation of the millennial reign of Christ described in Revelation chapter 20. The Text speaks of Satan being bound for a thousand years and Christ reigning with the saints during that time period. We read in Revelation 20:4-6:

> *I saw thrones on which were seated those who had been given authority to judge. And I saw the souls of those who had been beheaded because of their testimony about Jesus and because of the word of God. They had not worshiped the beast or its image and had not received its mark on their foreheads or their hands. They came to life and reigned with Christ a thousand years. (The rest of the dead did not come to life until the thousand years were ended.) This is the first resurrection. Blessed and holy are those who share in the first resurrection. The second death has no power over them, but they will be priests of God and of Christ and will reign with him for a thousand years.*

How one understands these verses (and thus the nature of the millennial reign of Christ) depends on how one views Revelation as a whole. Is Revelation a description of future events? Is it a symbolic message communicating timeless truth about the Gospel? Are the visions of John in Revelation concerning events that have already occurred? Such interpretive questions have existed since the first few centuries of the Christian Church.[16]

---

[16] Craig R. Koester, *Revelation and the End of All Things*, 2nd ed. (Grand Rapids, MI: William B. Eerdmans Publishing Company, 2018), 2.

Folio from Flemish Apocalypse, circa 1400.
Note the rising of the saints to reign with Christ.

Indeed, the millennium has been an important concept in theology since the early Church. It is not seen as an insignificant period of time but as a restored earthly kingdom in which Jesus reigns with the saints. This time period is seen as an intermediate period between the broken world that we now live in and our eternal state of Heaven. It is a prelude to what follows. This period is often referred to as "the golden age." The early Church Bishop Irenaeus held to the belief in a literal millennial kingdom before the Final Judgment and Heaven. He argued that since

Jesus promised His disciples that they would drink wine with Him again in His Father's Kingdom[17], then there must be a physical reign of Christ on earth one day.[18] Millennial thinking was popular in the early Church but became essentially dormant during the Middle Ages. It has had a renewed focus in the last few centuries with it being an important piece of Protestant theology.

What you decide to do with the millennium determines which eschatological camp you fall into. You may wonder how the interpretation of a handful of verses develops into various perspectives on the end-times. As I have described, people bring their own context and outlook to the interpretive table. New Testament Professor Craig Koester writes regarding the millennial interpretation: "The vision of the millennial kingdom is intriguing, in part, because it leaves so much to the imagination that readers inevitably disclose their own ideas when they explain what they think the passage means."[19] The major millennial positions are often a combination of one's interpretive method for Revelation, one's prior eschatological beliefs, and one's context altogether. I now turn to offer a brief overview of the millennial positions so that we can arrive at a better understanding of how the doctrine of the rapture fits into eschatological thinking.[20]

Postmillennialism

This belief holds that Jesus Christ will return after the millennial period (the golden age). You may wonder how Christ can reign for a millennium[21] if He returns at the end of it. Good question! Postmillennialism holds that Christ reigns spiritually during that time period. After the golden age is complete, Christ then

---

[17] Cf. Matthew 26:29

[18] Alister E. McGrath, *Christian Theology: An Introduction*, 4th ed. (Malden: Blackwell Publ, 2007), 480.

[19] Koester, *Revelation,* 3.

[20] I struggled with whether or not to offer a concise summary of these views. Please know that each of these views has its own history and its own sub-classes with smaller differences between its adherents. Just as there is a full taxonomy of organisms in the world, perhaps someone could design a taxonomy that classifies all the various eschatologies in Christian theology.

[21] Some followers of this view do not believe it is for a literal 1,000 years but an indefinite, long period of time.

comes physically to the earth followed by the Final Judgment. During the golden age, the Holy Spirit is at work in the world bringing about mass transformation: the Gospel is spread throughout the world, many are converted, nations and societies embrace Christian principles, and the world looks more and more like Heaven.[22]

This eschatological viewpoint is one of optimism. It believes that God's work in the world is so great so as to establish a period of time on earth so wonderful that it can be said to be supernaturally ruled by Christ. Postmillennialism was very popular in the 1600s through the end of the 1800s.[23] This theological position was reinforced by the general optimism of the time period. During this era, great advancements were made in virtually every field around the world. Great Kingdom

---

[22] Grenz, *The Millennial Maze*, 70-71. I read this entire book, and it is the best book for understanding millennial perspectives. If you want to know more about all of the different millennial positions, you must read this book. Granted, the book is a little dated, but we are looking at Christian thought which spans "a few years."
[23] Grenz, 66.

work was witnessed in the First and Second Great Awakenings (Mid 1700s and late 1700s lasting for a few decades), the Businessmen's Revival (1857-1858), and the Azusa Street Revival (1906). Largely due to the atrocities of the world in the 20th century, postmillennialism has greatly waned, and a more pessimistic view of the world is held.[24]

John misunderstood what was meant by "millennial speed dating." His first date, a postmillennial named Patricia, repeatedly talked about preterism and what life would be like for her two dogs in the golden age.

Amillennialism

Adherents of this view do not believe in a literal 1,000-year reign of Christ on the earth. Amillennialism does not ignore or disregard the millennium in Revelation. Rather, it is interpreted either symbolically or as a vision of the eternal Kingdom

---

[24] This makes sense when you reflect upon the horrors that the world witnessed in the 1900s: two World Wars, the development and use of the atomic bomb, the Holocaust, genocide, the Cold War, etc. In light of such things, it became increasingly difficult to see how the world can be transformed without a physical appearance of Christ.

of God.[25] Thus, when Christ returns to the earth, resurrections will occur, the Last Judgment will take place, and then believers enter into eternity with the Lord. Unlike the other views, there is no Golden Age on earth nor is there a focus on end-time chronologies. Amillennialism simply upholds the plain truths revealed in the New Testament on what will happen when Christ returns.

Interestingly, this was the dominant eschatological view for most of Christian history. From the time of Saint Augustine (roughly 400 AD) to well after the Protestant Reformation, amillennialism was the typical eschatological outlook. Knowledge of Church history helps us to understand why this was the case. In the 300s, Christianity was legalized in the Roman Empire and later announced as the official state religion. With the spread of the Gospel along with its firm foundation out of the ashes out of the Roman Empire, Christianity became institutionalized in the Western World. Over these centuries, eschatology was not a prominent concern since the Church had so much stability.[26] With the Christian faith so firmly established, with no obvious threats to its demise, the idea of a millennial reign of Christ was not seen as essential.[27] There are still many adherents of this view today including Roman Catholics[28] and many Protestant believers.

Premillennialism

This perspective holds that Jesus Christ shall return before the start of the millennial golden age. As opposed to postmillennialism, Jesus will physically appear and reign over the world during that time period. There are two branches

---

[25] Grenz, 26. There are many different understandings of how those in the amillennial camp understand Revelation 20. One view is that the current age of the Church is the millennium talked about. Yet, all amillennialists believe in the truth of this passage...they just don't hold to a literal interpretation.

[26] McGrath, *Christian Theology*, 481.

[27] With the Pope wielding so much power already, why would Jesus need to have an earthly reign?

[28] DS 3839 of the Roman Catholic Church denounces a literal millennial rule of Christ. Thus, the Catholic Church embraces amillennialism. See also Article 7, paragraphs 675-677 of the Catechism of the Catholic Church.

of premillennialism: Historical Premillennialism and Dispensationalism.[29] Characteristic of both branches are the following beliefs: Jesus shall return, He will judge the antichrist, Satan will be bound, the righteous will be resurrected, there will be a period of great tribulation on the earth, true believers will be raptured, there will be an earthly reign of Christ, a subsequent resurrection for the wicked, after which will be the Final Judgment.[30]

It is in the taxonomy of premillennialism where our focus on the rapture is located. In this field, Christ shall come and rapture the believers before the onset of the millennium. There are significant differences between the two branches. Historic premillennialism is so-called historic since it traces its roots back to the patristic period (first few centuries of the Church).[31] Historic Premillennialism holds that the eschatological focus is on the Christian Church[32] while Dispensationalism holds that the eschatological focus is on Israel.[33]

Dispensationalism was developed by Rev. John Darby, a minister from the Church of Ireland in the early 1800s. Darby brought this particular form of Premillennialism to the United States, and it spread like wildfire. By the middle of the 20th century, it was the dominant eschatology for evangelical and fundamentalist Christians in the country.[34] This eschatological position still holds strong today. Indeed, this eschatological view has invaded our collective consciousness, especially regarding the rapture.

---

[29] I know...a lot of big words. I am at least making it easier by shortening Dispensational Premillennialism to Dispensationalism.
[30] Grenz, *The Millennial Maze*, 128-129.
[31] Grenz, 26.
[32] Understanding that God's work for Israel in the OT switches over to the Church in the NT, composed of both Jews and Gentiles. Romans 10:4 good buddy!
[33] Grenz, 98.
[34] Grenz, 91.

There are several distinctive tenets of dispensationalism that stand out from the other views[35]:

- The history of God's saving work in the world is divided into seven[36] eras or dispensations (hence the title dispensationalism). In these various eras, God relates differently to mankind through His revelation and man's responsibility.

- A futuristic, literal hermeneutic in approaching the Bible. This is especially true of the prophecies in the Bible (both Old and New Testaments). For example, key passages from the book of Daniel are often viewed as providing specific guidance and chronologies on what is to come in the future.

- The Second Coming of Jesus will take place in two parts. The first will occur when all Christians are raptured (taken away), leaving behind on the earth only non-Christians and Israel. At this point, only raptured Christians will see Jesus. After the time of the great tribulation, which lasts for 7 years, Jesus shall make His "second Second Coming," but this one will be public. At this point Jesus will reign on the earth physically in the Millennial Kingdom, the Golden Age.

- There is a pronounced distinction between Israel and the Church (that is, Christians). Both are viewed as God's people, but Israel is understood as God's national people and the Church is God's spiritual people.[37] The Church is saved through the Gospel message (grace through faith in Jesus), but the nation of Israel is saved and blessed immensely during the Golden age. As I mentioned earlier, the eschatological focus of dispensationalism is on Israel. The Church is not present during the seven years of the Tribulation. While the Church is generally believed to be present during the Millennial reign of Christ on

---

[35] George Lyons, "Premillennialism," essay, in *Beacon Dictionary of Theology*, ed. Richard S. Taylor, J. Kenneth Grider, and Willard H. Taylor (Kansas City, Mo: Beacon Hill Press of Kansas City, 1983), 414.

[36] Not all view the number as seven, but the majority do.

[37] Another way to think about it is this: Israel is God's earthly people, but the Church is God's heavenly people.

earth (returning to the earth with Jesus), the focus during the Golden
Age is on Israel, during which God will complete all the prophecies
concerning them from the Old Testament.

Both of these branches of premillennialism hold that the believers will be removed
from the world prior to the tribulation. This aspect of premillennial thought, the
rapture, led to my fear of being taken away from the earth in 1999. It is
premillennialism's understanding of the rapture, especially its understanding in
dispensationalism, that forms the focus of the remainder of this chapter.

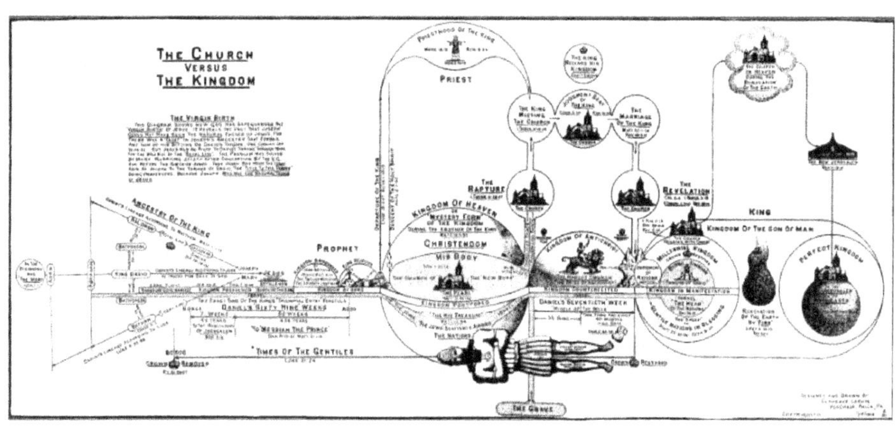

An illustrated timetable showing the intricacies of dispensationalism.
By Clarence Larkin, 1918.

RAPTURE IN THE NEW TESTAMENT AND OUR USE OF THE WORD

The word "rapture" will not be found in any decent translation of the Bible. The
word for rapture in the English language is derived from the Latin word *Rapio*,
which literally means to seize, take hold by force, or carry away.[38] We get this
modern word of rapture because Saint Jerome used this word in the Vulgate to
translate the Greek word ἁρπάζω/harpazo. This word is used in 1 Thessalonians

---

[38] The word "raptor" also has the same etymological origin as it describes birds of prey
who snatch up their food or dinosaurs who steal their next meal.

4:17, where the believers are caught up to meet the Lord in the air. As we will look at later, this is a popular verse that is believed to describe the event known as the rapture.

Our main concern is how the Greek word ἁρπάζω/harpazo is used in the New Testament. If we want to understand what the rapture is, it is necessary to know what it means and how it is used in the New Testament. Harpazo carries the same essential meaning as the Latin word rapio, meaning to catch (away, up), snatch, or carry off. It is used 14 times in the New Testament; Some references with good connotations for snatching and some with bad connotations. In 2 Corinthians 12:2-4, Paul is "caught up" to the third heaven/paradise where he receives special revelation from the Lord.[39] Likewise, in Acts 8:39, Philip is snatched away by the Holy Spirit after baptizing the Ethiopian Eunuch. The same Greek word is used negatively at times to refer to the actions of the evil one snatching away (Matthew 13:19) or snatching believers out of Jesus' hands (John 10:28). Out of all the times ἁρπάζω/harpazo is used in the New Testament, it is only used once in connection with the Second Coming of Christ (1 Thessalonians 4:17). Since it only has one appearance related to Jesus' return to earth, the word does not have a strong foundation in the New Testament in an eschatological sense. Despite this fact, it does not mean the rapture is not a biblical doctrine. The word "Trinity" never appears in the Bible, but the Church has recognized the doctrine of the Trinity as a central tenet of the faith. The question to consider is if the concept of the rapture is articulated in the Bible.

It is best to come to clarify the terms we are using. Have you ever had a disagreement with someone only to eventually realize that the problem was a lack of clarification or a lack of a mutual understanding of terms?[40] The rapture may be understood differently depending on who is using the term. Of course, someone may understand rapture as simply what Paul says happens in 1 Thessalonians 4:17: that the believers are caught up with the Lord in the air. Fair enough. But when

---

[39] The Text says that Paul is speaking about a man in Christ, but most scholars believe he is speaking about himself.

[40] My brother and I once had an argument based on different ideas on what a "door prize" is.

most people use the word, even if they are referring to that specific verse, they have a certain idea of what that looks like. Dispensationalists hold that the rapture will be a "secret rapture." This understanding of the rapture holds that only the believers will see Christ as they are whisked away (either going into the air or vanishing). The entire world will only see Christ at His Second Coming (this is often referred to as the *Parousia*—a Greek word meaning presence. Parousia thus refers to the second part of Christ's return in dispensationalism). Other premillennialists understand the rapture as a removal of the believers at another point in time.[41]

Others define rapture as what happens to believers at the Parousia. One pertinent example comes from biblical scholar Douglas Moo.[42] He understands rapture, not as vanishing or going away to heaven, but as bodily transformation when Christ returns. While the deceased saints are resurrected, living believers are "raptured" or instantaneously receiving a new, incorruptible body in order to properly receive God's eternal Kingdom.[43] This definition of rapture would see 1 Corinthians 15:51-53 as a rapture Text.[44] Many interpreters view this bodily transformation as included in the rapture—both the removal of the person from the earth and then the transformation. All may not use the term in the same way, but it is important to know what definition we are working with when discussing it. The definition I am working with is the one that appears to be the most widely used—that of

---

[41] There are a lot of subclasses in premillennialism which are classified by when the rapture will occur. These common views are: pre-trib, mid-trib, post-trib partial rapturism, and pre-wrath.

[42] Moo is a premillennialist that believes Christ will come after the tribulation (post-trib).

[43] Alan Hultberg, Craig A. Blaising, and Douglas J. Moo, *Three Views on the Rapture: Pretribulation, Prewrath, or Posttribulation*, 2nd ed. (Grand Rapids, Mich: Zondervan, 2010), 185-186. Moo further elucidates on the rapture by clarifying that it is not a removal for believers but a joining together with the Lord.

[44] 1 Cor. 15:51-53: "Listen, I tell you a mystery: We will not all sleep, but we will all be changed— in a flash, in the twinkling of an eye, at the last trumpet. For the trumpet will sound, the dead will be raised imperishable, and we will be changed. For the perishable must clothe itself with the imperishable, and the mortal with immortality."

believers being instantly transported away from the earth while the rest of the world remains (likely experiencing the bodily transformation in the process).

Rapture History and Interpretation.

Does the Bible teach this particular understanding of the rapture? The answer to that depends on who you ask! Some interpreters regard the rapture as a biblical doctrine that is clearly outlined in the Bible, but admitting that few people readily understood it until its articulation by Darby in the 19th century. Other interpreters see no evidence in the Bible for the rapture, arguing that the rapture did not exist until it was created by Darby. Is the rapture a newly created doctrine? Or is it a doctrine that was neglected or overlooked throughout the ages? In an article entitled "The Rapture in Twenty Centuries of Biblical Interpretation," James Stitzinger looks at the history of this doctrine and in church history. However, his survey of church history doesn't yield any significant fruit until you get to Darby in the 1800s. The doctrine is really not found in writing in the first few centuries of the Church. Stitzinger freely admits, "In the end, no one can produce a clear statement of patristic eschatology regarding the rapture."[45] Perhaps the earliest reference to the rapture is from Pseudo-Ephraem circa 373.[46] Before this, there is no clear indication of the early Church Fathers writing or teaching about the rapture. Furthermore, for nearly a millennium after Pseudo-Ephraem's eschatological proclamation, rapture discussion is essentially nil. Advocates of the rapture position may still argue that the doctrine is true but lacked proper development. This is possible. After all, it took the Church a few centuries until a proper Christology was fully developed and articulated. On the other hand, perhaps reading the rapture in biblical texts is an example of the Humpty Dumpty Effect.

Let us examine three passages of Scripture that are commonly seen as exhibiting the rapture.

---

[45] James F Stitzinger, "The Rapture in Twenty Centuries of Biblical Interpretation," *The Master's Seminary Journal* 13, no. 2 (2002): 149–71, 156.
[46] Stitzinger, 157.

> *Do not let your hearts be troubled. You believe in God;*
> *believe also in me. My Father's house has many rooms; if*
> *that were not so, would I have told you that I am going*
> *there to prepare a place for you? And if I go and prepare a*
> *place for you, I will come back and take you to be with me*
> *that you also may be where I am.*
> (John 14:1-3)

In these verses, Jesus is speaking to His disciples and comforting them before He goes to the cross. While the immediate context is not eschatological in nature, Jesus states that He will prepare a place for the disciples and then return and take the disciples to be with Him. What does Jesus mean by this? Is he talking about gathering the disciples together immediately after His resurrection (but before His ascension)? Does Jesus refer to the Second Coming? Or the arrival of the Holy Spirit? Some see in this passage an implicit teaching of the rapture. That is, Jesus taking the disciples to be with Him is being raptured. This is the viewpoint of theology professor Craig Blaising. He argues for a pretribulation rapture, saying that the believers taken to be with Jesus is similar to 1 Thessalonians 4:17.[47] Douglas Moo understands Jesus' promise in these verses as His returning, but not our definition of rapture. Moo argues that there is no indication of when He will return in these verses.[48] Many biblical scholars agree with Moo that Jesus refers to His Second Coming in this passage but not a specific mention of when or how.[49]

The context makes it most likely that Jesus is referring to His Second Coming. In preparing a place for His disciples, He makes a way for all who believe in Him to go to the Father and to abide in His presence for eternity. Though Jesus' statement likely refers to His return to earth, John's Gospel holds no specific eschatological timeline in these verses. To insert one, or to declare that John speaks about a secret rapture, is to read into the Text your own eschatology. All in all, Jesus' message in these verses is one of encouragement and comfort to His disciples. He will leave,

---

[47] Blaising, *Three Views on the Rapture*, 249-250.

[48] Moo, *Three Views on the Rapture*, 197.

[49] Reading over commentaries, this seems to be the majority opinion.

but He will return one day and bring them into the Father's Presence (though the Text does not elaborate on the specifics of it).

> *But about that day or hour no one knows, not even the angels in heaven, nor the Son, but only the Father. As it was in the days of Noah, so it will be at the coming of the Son of Man. For in the days before the flood, people were eating and drinking, marrying and giving in marriage, up to the day Noah entered the ark; and they knew nothing about what would happen until the flood came and took them all away. That is how it will be at the coming of the Son of Man. Two men will be in the field; one will be taken and the other left. Two women will be grinding with a hand mill; one will be taken and the other left.*
> (Matthew 24:36-41)

The final two verses of this passage have been popularly understood as illustrating the rapture. The common perception of this scene is that while two people are together, the righteous one is immediately raptured to Heaven while the wicked one remains. But do these verses actually teach the rapture? If not, what is Jesus talking about?

Matthew 24-25 is called the Olivet Discourse, deriving from Jesus speaking on the Mount of Olives. This is one of the most difficult passages to interpret in the Gospels. Without branching off and possibly starting another chapter, which I am sure you would be THRILLED ABOUT, it shall be sufficient to share a couple of things about the chapter to put our two verses in the appropriate context. This chapter has largely been interpreted in three ways: as a prediction of 1st century events associated with the destruction of the Temple,[50] events that will happen

---

[50] In 70 AD, the Romans placed a siege on Jerusalem. The Temple was destroyed; thousands of Jews were killed or displaced. It was a terrible, bloody war that reshaped the nature of Judaism. Jesus may have been speaking about these specific things to come.

shortly near and at the Second Coming, or a combination of the former two.[51] If the reader views the passage as any of the latter two options, then the verses quoted are definitely eschatological in nature. From my perspective, the majority of interpreters of our Text view it as a reference to events surrounding Jesus' Second Coming, with many having the rapture in mind in verses 40-41.

"Rapture: one at the mill," by Jan Luyken - Bowyer's Bible, Bolton, England.

Working with the popular interpretation that the verses quoted are eschatological, let us examine what Jesus is saying and see if the rapture is being taught here. The immediate context shows us that Jesus is talking about the coming of the Son of Man (Himself). It is emphasized that nobody knows when His arrival will take place. Jesus reinforces this point by stating that while people are going about their normal business, one person will be taken, and one will be left behind. The Text is clear on this point. What is not as clear is which one is righteous: the one taken

---

[51] Douglas Moo, *Three Views of the Rapture*, 212-213.

or the one left behind. While interpreting the passage as the righteous being taken away is natural for rapture advocates, I argue that the proper reading is that the righteous are left behind while the wicked are taken away (for judgment).[52]

The context of these verses favors this interpretation. Jesus offers a comparison between Noah's generation and the people at the return of the Son of Man. The Lord spares Noah and his family on the ark while the wicked are taken away by the flood. In setting these two groups of people side by side, Jesus shows us that it is the righteous who are saved, that is, left behind. We wouldn't say that Noah and his family were "taken away" on the ark. Rather, in judgment, the wicked are washed away or taken away by the flood.[53] It wouldn't make sense for Jesus to flip his analogy between the two parties. Rather, the Text shows that the wicked are taken away while the righteous are spared/left behind.[54] Matthew's Gospel as a whole also confirms this reading. Consider the parable of the weeds that Jesus gives in Matthew 13. The wheat and the weeds are together, but it is the weeds which are taken away and burned. The righteous/wheat are left behind to "shine like the sun in the kingdom of their Father."[55] Furthermore, a few verses after the passage in question, Jesus shares an illustration about faithful and wicked servants left in charge of their master's household (13:46-51). The faithful and wise servant is not taken away when the master returns but is rewarded by remaining and receiving

---

[52] Being taken with mom to run errands is like punishment, but being left behind at home to play video games is good.

[53] Benjamin L. Merkle, "Who Will Be Left Behind? Rethinking the Meaning of Matthew 24:40-41 and Luke 17:34-35," *Westminster Theological Journal* 72 (2010): 169–79, 174. I highly recommend Merkle's article. He provides a great analysis of this passage.

[54] Some biblical commentators have argued that the Greek verb used in Matthew 24:40-41, παραλαμβάνω/ paralambanó, is used to connote salvation. They refer to other instances of the word, such as in John 14:3 where Jesus takes His disciples with Him into the Father's presence, and how it is used in a positive sense. While the same word is used in John 14:3, the truth is that paralambanó is ambiguous enough that it doesn't inherently carry any significance. It simply means to take with oneself. It is found approximately 50 times in the New Testament, not including cognates. It is found in both positive and negative contexts. Some negative examples include the devil taking Jesus with him and the soldiers taking Jesus to be crucified. With all this in mind, no solid argument can be made for interpreting paralambanó as specifically good or bad. It depends on its immediate context.

[55] Matthew 13:43.

more responsibility. The wicked servant receives a terrible fate. He is cut into pieces and assigned a place with the hypocrites. While the words "taken away" are not used, the wicked servant no longer remains there (in one piece or many!).

A common pattern of judgment and salvation in the Old Testament also supports this interpretation of our Text. A pattern is established in the Old Testament where the wicked are either taken away or destroyed but the righteous are left behind.[56] Consider the Lord's people's great punishment in the Old Testament, the exile. They are taken away from their land. Removal here is definitely punishment, not reward. Furthermore, many passages reinforce this notion. Isaiah 4:2-4 shares how the survivors in Israel shall be called holy, yet the filth will be washed away. Likewise, consider the prophecy found in Zephaniah 3:11-12:

> *On that day you, Jerusalem, will not be put to shame*
> *for all the wrongs you have done to me,*
> *because I will remove from you*
> *your arrogant boasters.*
> *Never again will you be haughty*
> *on my holy hill.*
> *But I will leave within you*
> *the meek and humble.*
> *The remnant of Israel*
> *will trust in the name of the Lord.*

The Lord removes the arrogant and wicked but leaves behind a holy remnant. As we can see, both the immediate context of Matthew 24 and biblical context as a whole support the idea that the righteous are the ones left behind.

---

[56] Merkle, 170.

Brothers and sisters, we do not want you to be uninformed about those who sleep in death, so that you do not grieve like the rest of mankind, who have no hope. For we believe that Jesus died and rose again, and so we believe that God will bring with Jesus those who have fallen asleep in him. According to the Lord's word, we tell you that we who are still alive, who are left until the coming of the Lord, will certainly not precede those who have fallen asleep. For the Lord himself will come down from heaven, with a loud command, with the voice of the archangel and with the trumpet call of God, and the dead in Christ will rise first. After that, we who are still alive and are left will be caught up together with them in the clouds to meet the Lord in the air. And so we will be with the Lord forever. Therefore encourage one another with these words.

(1 Thessalonians 4:13-18)

This Text is the focal passage for those who hold to the doctrine of the rapture. As mentioned earlier, this passage contains the Greek word ἁρπάζω/harpazo from which we get our English word "rapture." Many dispensationalists and premillennialists use this passage as evidence for the doctrine. Consider what Charles Ryrie, a dispensationalist, writes concerning this passage: "His coming here is *in the air*, not to the earth, and will occur just prior to the beginning of the tribulation period (see Rev. 3:10). That period will end with His coming to the earth."[57] Including this statement as a study note alongside the Scripture Text, Ryrie comments on the two-part nature of Christ's return in line with dispensationalism. He also mentions the tribulation. Yet, an honest assessment of the Text understands that neither the tribulation nor a subsequent return of Jesus is specified in this passage. It makes logical sense for someone who believes in the

---

[57] Charles Caldwell Ryrie, *The Ryrie Study Bible: New American Standard Translation: With Introductions, Annotations, Outlines, Marginal References, Harmony of the Gospels, Synopsis of Bible Doctrine, Index of Scripture, Index to Notes, Concordance, Maps, and Timeline Charts and Many Other Helps* (Chicago: Moody Press, 1978), 1809.

rapture to read that doctrine in line with this passage. After all, it does mention Christ and believers meeting in the air. But does this passage teach the so-called rapture?[58]

The best aid for interpretation is the immediate context of the Scripture passage. If a passage is unclear, a student of God's Word ought to try to understand it first and foremost in its own textual situation. The gist of what Paul is writing in 1 Thessalonians 4:13-18 is encouragement and hope based on proper Christian eschatology. We need to keep this in mind when reading this passage. Paul is not highlighting every detail of the end-times. He is writing to the believers in Thessalonica who are worried about their fellow church members who have passed away. Since they believed in the imminence of Christ's return, the believers were unsure about the fate of those who died. Will they receive eternal inheritance? Will they get to witness the Lord's return and be present? Paul addresses such questions.[59]

In its literary context, Paul is addressing these eschatological concerns regarding the deceased believers. Notice what Paul highlights in these verses. Christians are different from the world; we do not grieve the same way. Those who are alive when Jesus returns will not have any advantage over the deceased. The dead in Christ will rise, and all will be present to greet our Lord Jesus in the air. Paul brackets this section by references to Christian hope and encouragement. In verse 13, Paul writes that he does not want the believers to grieve without hope like the world. In the conclusion of this section, he writes, "Therefore encourage one another with these words." With these things in mind, we see that Paul's focus in not on the

---

[58] The argument that this passage teaches the rapture because the rapture is in it is circular reasoning. In studying the Text, we attempt to understand exactly what Paul meant when he wrote these words. We have already viewed how the word ἁρπάζω/harpazo is used in other places.

[59] It may strike us as odd today that they would wonder such things, but our eschatological expectation has changed in the last couple of millennia. If we strongly believed that Jesus would return within the next year and someone passed, we would wonder the same things if we didn't have an established eschatology yet.

how of Christ's return or of the rapture per se, but his focus is on the hope that all believers, living or dead, have in Christ for when He returns.[60]

If the focus of this passage is on eschatological comfort for the believers, how should we understand the meeting of the saints with the Lord in the air? Some Bible scholars and theologians argue that Paul's description of meeting with Christ in the air ought to not be understood in a strict, literal sense.[61] The late scholar William Barclay regards Paul's eschatological description as poetic and an attempt to describe the indescribable. He remarks, "We are not meant to take with crude and insensitive literalism what is a seer's vision."[62] While not expressed in the same manner, Bible scholar N. T. Wright also suggests that these verses ought not be understood as a literal depiction of the Second Coming. Rather, they are Paul's way (with a slightly confusing mix of metaphors and stories) of explaining what occurs at the Parousia.[63] What we know about Jesus' return to earth is that He will descend from the sky (the reverse of His ascension in Acts chapter 1). Like many other things foretold in Scripture, the details are not all spelled out. But as Paul mentions in these verses, the believers will meet the Lord in the air. Yet, this does not indicate that Christ is removing the believers while allowing the wicked to remain (i.e. rapture).

Paul's language in these verses sheds some light on the "meeting" between the Lord and the Christians in the air.[64] The Greek word for meeting used in verse 17 is

---

[60] The previously referenced Bible scholar Douglas Moo agrees with my statements here. His analysis of this passage shows that Paul's focus is on the comfort that all believers will meet Christ. Furthermore, evidence for removal of believers before tribulation or a two-part return of Christ is not found in this passage. Moo, *Three Views on the Rapture*, 198-200.

[61] That doesn't mean it's not a physical return of Christ...just not the literal and specific details used here.

[62] William Barclay, *The Letters to the Philippians, Colossians, and Thessalonians* (Philadelphia: Westminster Press, 1975), 203.

[63] N. T. Wright, *Surprised by Hope* (New York: HarperOne, 2018), 143-144. According to Wright, 1 Thess. 4:16-17 is a different way of stating what Paul writes in 1 Cor. 15:23-27, 51-54, and Philippians 3:20-21. I would recommend the reader to read his book for the full description. It is well-written.

[64] Does Phil Collins' song "In the Air Tonight" talk about the Second Coming? Hmm...

ἀπάντησις/apantēsis. The word presents the Greco-Roman custom of meeting or welcoming a very important person (think magistrate or emperor or even me!). To welcome the cherished visitor, it was customary to go out to welcome him and then escort the visitor back into the city/destination.[65] We can certainly understand this concept. If you are picking up your significant other from the airport, should you wait in the parking lot while playing games on your phone? NO! You meet your beloved at baggage claim and carry their bags back to the car.[66] You go out to welcome the special person. The implication is that the initial meeting spot is not where the two parties remain. Given this understanding, it is fair to imagine or interpret that Christ and the believers return to earth after initially meeting in the air.[67] The Text doesn't specify what happens after the meeting. Yet, as I have explained, Paul's focus is on comfort and hope; he is not laying out all the details of the Second Coming. All things considered, this passage does not teach the rapture but provides hope for the believers in Jesus' return.

The three passages I have investigated have often been interpreted as passages about the rapture, but my analysis shows that they do not support the doctrine. As the reader has been able to see throughout the book, the Humpty Dumpty Effect has caused many to view such passages as speaking about the rapture even though many statements are vague (such as John 14:1-3 where Jesus promises to come back again). I again implore the reader to approach eschatological texts with fresh eyes—to hold an openness to the Text without trying to read into it whichever eschatological viewpoint you currently hold. When we do that, we may find something new—such as Jesus' message in Matthew 24 about the wicked being taken away while the righteous remain.

As I wrap up this final chapter of the book, I would like to offer one concluding idea for the reader to consider—the nature of our eschatological hope. The New

---

[65] Matthew Dickerson, "Who Gets Left Behind?," *Christianity Today*, June 2011, 41. Others reference this understanding of the Greek word including Wright and Moo.
[66] Also, midwestern hospitality suggests that when family or dear friends come to your house, you greet them at the door and stand there and talk for a while. The same thing happens upon departure. On some occasions, this may last for hours.
[67] I wonder how we will get up in the air. Jet packs?

Testament repeatedly admonishes believers to be ready for the return of Christ but to do in hope. The return of Jesus and all that will transpire should give us a comforting hope. But what is the exact nature of this hope? Is our hope on the destruction of our current fallen world? Is our hope on the expectation of rapture (that is, removal) from the physical world and brought somewhere else? I would humbly suggest that these options are inferior to what the Lord intends for us. Instead of removal, God opts for rescue and renewal. Instead of destruction, God promises re-creation and resurrection.

We should consider the theological implications of an eschatological hope centered on the Lord removing us from the physical world and brought into an eternal state of disembodiment. God's creation is good (cf. Genesis 1). It is marred because of the entrance of sin, but it is still good and valuable to the Lord. This includes our physical bodies. Jesus' resurrection shows that our bodies will not be eliminated but renewed, raised incorruptible…and they will still be physical bodies. We won't be angelic spirits floating on clouds and playing harps.[68]

God is great enough to restore and renew what He has originally made rather than trash it and start again. Allow me to offer an illustration. One New Year's Eve I made plans to make my wife-to-be a delicious meal. I decided to make roast duck with all the appropriate sides. I couldn't wait to surprise her with a delicious meal as she came over to my apartment. Unfortunately, my culinary skills did not match my love for her. The duck was not fully thawed so I had to resolve that issue. Then, I realized that I did not have the right cookware for roast duck. This led to the smoke alarm going off as butter dripped off the tiny pan and burned on the bottom of the oven. The end result was the partially cooked duck being thrown into the dumpster behind the building and ordering pizza.

God's plan doesn't involve the metaphorical equivalent of throwing creation into the dumpster and ordering pizza. God loves His creation and wants to renew it. This is God's plan of redemption—to save, redeem, and restore the world through Jesus Christ. Of course, God will deal with evil and that wily serpent. That is

---

[68] I don't know who created that expression of eternity. It's not enticing…it's pretty lame.

certainly part of God's plan at the eschaton. But to think of salvation as removal from the world is more in line with Platonic or Gnostic thought rather than what is stated in the Bible.[69] N. T. Wright states that "the New Testament, true to its Old Testament roots, regularly insists that the major, central, framing question is that of God's purpose of rescue and re-creation for the whole world, the entire cosmos."[70] If Jesus were physically present in my smoky kitchen that New Year's Eve, He would have been able to correct my mistakes and prepare that roast duck. He would have redeemed it rather than throwing it in the dumpster. It is in this understanding of God's work that we find our hope—God's ability and promise to renew, restore, and resurrect all of creation.[71]

Wading through the various eschatological viewpoints and trying to understand what will occur at the end is overwhelming. While there is definitely space for loving dialogue on eschatology (as I have expressed my views in this book), our ultimate hope isn't on our own eschatological stance per se. We may look forward to the golden age, or we may not believe in a literal millennial reign of Christ. We may believe in separate plans for the Christian Church and Israel, or we may believe there is only one Church and God's plan for it. We may dismiss all of these options and simply cling to pan-millennialism.[72] Our ultimate hope is in the Lord Himself and His promise of resurrection and a glorious future. It's alright if we don't know all the eschatological details. What matters most is that we know and trust the Lord. I believe the words from Daniel Whittle's hymn from the 19th century say it best for all of us.

---

[69] This thought is echoed by Matthew Dickerson (previously cited). Psalm 139 reflects upon the wonder of our bodies and states that we are fearfully and wonderfully made. Also, if God's plan did not seek renewal and restoration on earth, why did Jesus' ministry involve so much physical healing? Jesus' healing is a foretaste of what is to come!

[70] Wright, *Surprised by Hope*, 197.

[71] Scriptures such as Romans 8:18-27, 1 Cor. 15, and Revelation 21:1-8 are great reminders of these truths.

[72] All things will "pan out" in the end if I trust in the Lord.

"I know not when my Lord may come,
at night or noon-day fair,
nor if I'll walk the vale with him,
or meet him in the air.
"But 'I know whom I have believed,
and am persuaded that he is able
to keep that which I've committed
unto him against that day.'"

CONLUSION

•

I want to thank the reader for persevering through this book and arriving here. What a journey it has been! We started in the garden and finished with the return of our Lord while looking at our interpretive habits along the way. I hope by now you can understand what the Humpty Dumpty Effect is and how it affects our interpretation of the Word of God. We Christians recognize the authority of the Word of God, and we need to respect this wonderful form of revelation that the Lord has given to us. One way that we can all do that is by being mindful of the Humpty Dumpty Effect and being good students of the Bible. Now, I recognize that some instances of the Humpty Dumpty Effect are minor and almost insignificant. A couple of examples would be Saul falling off a donkey (instead of simply falling to the ground) or Mary riding on a donkey to Bethlehem.[1] I doubt any serious theological issues would develop by reading these narratives in that manner. Yet, it is always best to be true and faithful to the Text as presented because details do matter.

Some instances of the Humpty Dumpty Effect can be significant when interpretation deviates from the Bible's message. As I have shown throughout this book, the act of reading into a Text can lead us away from an accurate interpretation.[2] The Books of Samuel present David and Jonathan as loyal friends in difficult circumstances, not sexual lovers. The magi were never kings. The

---

[1] What is our fascination with donkeys???

[2] A poor interpretation may then lead to bad theology and bad actions.

doctrine of the rapture is on shaky ground and may lead to a theology that chooses escapism over renewal of creation. These are just a small sampling of the many interpretive errors that people can make. If we view the Word as God as true and authoritative, by God's grace we must be astute learners and read it properly.

With all this said, where do we go from here? Here are a few "big picture thoughts" in concluding this book.

The need for humility

One of my favorite professors from college would refer to himself as "extraordinarily humble." I have never determined if he was being sarcastic or sincere. Regardless, humility is a quality worth having. We ought to approach God's Word (and also the world) with a fair amount of humility. There is a lot we do not know. Even the smartest of us only hold a small thimble of knowledge compared to the vast oceans of information in the world. Remember the Pharisees and the Teachers of the Law from the Gospels? Sometimes we want to shout at them for getting it wrong. How can they be so stupid!? (I am being sarcastic). Remember, they were the smart guys of their age—and their lack of humility became a challenge to truly hear the Gospel from our Lord.

The Lord has humbled me in my life. It took me many years to realize that what I was so convinced of in the past was wrong. We should take heed of the many suggestions in Proverbs about the need for humility. In regard to the Word of God, we need to have humility when approaching the Text. I am not its Master, nor am I the master. The Text is the Message from the Master. Our duty as disciples is to humbly read, study, and obey what we find in the Holy Scriptures.

The Church needs a solid Christian epistemology

Just because this is the conclusion of the book does not mean that I cannot teach anything new. Epistemology is the study and theory of knowledge. It asks the deep philosophical questions like "How do I know what I know?" and "How do I know if something is true?" As Christians, we ought to hold an epistemology that holds up the Bible as authoritative and true. There's an old saying that says, "All truth is

God's truth." I find that to be very accurate. We gain knowledge (even spiritual knowledge) from many sources. Scientific study, tradition, reason/philosophy, experience, and even mathematics can provide knowledge. Yet, the revelation from the Word of God is special. It holds a sense of primacy in the area of spiritual knowledge. Imagine that all these sources of knowledge are anthropomorphized and they are sitting at a table. Each one has a voice, but Scripture sits at the head of the table, and its voice carries the most authority.

Commitment to biblical literacy

Though we have more access to the Bible than ever before in history, our society suffers from a lack of biblical literacy. As I demonstrated in the first chapter, many faithful Christians struggle to identify what popular sayings come from the Bible. Christianity is well-known in our current world, but fewer people know the details of the Christian faith and Bible well. A humorous anecdote illustrates this idea. Two men were discussing religion, with one claiming to be "very religious." The second gentlemen protested, "You are not that religious. I bet you $20 you cannot even say the Lord's Prayer." The first man proudly proclaimed, "Now I lay me down to sleep, I pray the Lord my soul to keep. And If I should die before I wake, I pray the Lord my soul to take." The other gentleman gave him $20 and confessed, "I was wrong. I didn't think you could do it." When our knowledge of God's Word is nominal, we may be inclined to make such a mistake.

A great need for the Church today is to have disciples learn the Bible more. Individuals and churches ought to seek creative ways to encourage believers to learn the Word. A key lay leader in my church recently created a verse of the month initiative for our congregation. The verse is shared on the first Sunday of the month, and people are encouraged to memorize the verse. Small printouts of the verse are provided so people can place them around their homes to learn the verse. Church-wide Bible reading programs are another popular way to encourage people to read the canon together. Since the Lord has made us creative beings, we ought to find new and interesting ways to promote the study of God's Word.[3] Regardless

---

[3] I once received my own pizza for memorizing the Gospel of John! I will say that the spiritual benefits have greatly outweighed the tasty meal.

of the methods we use, we need to remind people of the *why* behind studying the Bible. Texts such as 2 Timothy 3:16-17 and Hebrews 4:12 are great reminders of the significance and practical application for the Word of God.[4]

Living with uncertainty

I am a planner. I love planning out trips, giving great attention to where I will stay, where to eat, what to do, planning transportation, etc. For my last big vacation, I spent six months creating an itinerary for maximum enjoyment. I probably annoy my wife with my planning at times. I will ask her questions like, "What do you think we ought to do for dinner on the second Tuesday this month?" Planning is not a bad thing, but we cannot always plan as much as we would like since we don't know what details the future holds. For many of us, we don't have all the details that we would prefer. We would prefer to have the gaps filled in for our Bible narratives. We would prefer to think of the magi numbering three. We would prefer to have a detailed chronology of the end-times. Jesus reminds us that we do not know the day or hour of his return. Truth be told, there are a lot of things we don't know about the future.

Uncertainty plagues us. It prevents us from having complete exhaustive plans for the future. It plagues scientists when performing quantum measurements.[5] It may keep us awake at night as we strive to provide for our families. Even when uncertainty is built into something, we often don't like it. Have you ever read a story with an uncertain ending? In high school, I read the short story "The Birds" by Daphne du Maurier.[6] It is a good story, but the ending is intentionally vague. Will the family survive the upcoming attack from the birds? Nobody knows. The cliffhanger ending has always bothered me, but I have come to live with it.

---

[4] 2 Timothy 3:16-17: "All Scripture is God-breathed and is useful for teaching, rebuking, correcting and training in righteousness, so that the servant of God may be thoroughly equipped for every good work."
Hebrews 4:12: "For the word of God is alive and active. Sharper than any double-edged sword, it penetrates even to dividing soul and spirit, joints and marrow; it judges the thoughts and attitudes of the heart."
[5] Heisenberg Uncertainty Principle.
[6] This was later created into a movie, but I have never seen it.

Both in life in general and in our Christian faith, we need to live with some uncertainty. The Old Testament Patriarch Abraham is a wonderful example of how to live faithfully despite uncertainty. The Lord called him to leave his home and family and go to the land that He would later show him. I am sure Abraham (still called Abram at that time) had a thousand questions, but he trusted the Lord and went. We don't have all the details about the future or even about the Word of God. We may not know the number of magi, but we know the One whom the magi worshiped. Our ultimate calling as Christians is not to obtain perfect knowledge, but to trust in the Lord.

Thank you for your time and attention in reading *The Humpty Dumpty Effect*. This book took a long time to create, but it was worth it. With my manuscript now complete, I now begin making the exciting plans for my family and I to visit

APPENDIX: THE TROUBLE WITH THE INFANCY NARRATIVES

⸻ • ⸻

Perhaps trouble isn't the best word, but moving from the Nativity accounts in Matthew and Luke to a single Nativity scene is troublesome. As we have already read, people prefer to have a clean, detailed narrative with all of the gaps filled in. The relatively few details that we have about the birth of Jesus, however, make that difficult. As we consider the Nativity scene, there are two troublesome issues for the reader. The first one is with the chronology of Jesus' birth, His infancy, and the events surrounding it. Matthew and Luke present infancy narratives, but they don't contain all the same events. Here are the specific events from Matthew and Luke as they record what transpires and when.

Matthew:

Jesus is born to Mary in Bethlehem—no objective dates or events are given surrounding his birth.

Sometime after Jesus' birth, the magi arrive in Jerusalem asking about the one born king of the Jews.

King Herod sends the magi to Bethlehem.

The magi go to the house where Jesus is and worship Him. The magi depart back to their own country.

Joseph receives a message to take Mary and Jesus and flee to Egypt.

King Herod commands the murder of the infants in and around Bethlehem.

Luke:

Joseph and Mary travel from Nazareth to Bethlehem. While in Bethlehem, Jesus is born.

The angel of the Lord announces Jesus' birth to the shepherds; the shepherds go and see Jesus lying in the manger.

When Jesus is eight days old, He is circumcised-no location is given. This would not have been done at the Temple but in a home.

When Jesus is 40 days old, Mary and Joseph take Him to the Temple. They offer a sacrifice in accordance with the Law of Moses.

As you can see, there is not much overlap with the two accounts. They don't contradict one another but are complementary and focus on different events with Jesus' infancy. Altogether, arriving at a detailed chronology of Jesus' birth and infancy becomes difficult, especially concerning the magi…after all, the chapter in this book focuses on them.

There are many questions we can think of concerning the magi and the chronology: How does the magi narrative sync with Luke's account? When did the magi visit in respect of the shepherds? How old was Jesus when the magi visited? Did the magi visit before or after Jesus' family went to the Temple? All in all, it is best to take the accounts separately instead of trying to jam them together.[1]

The second troublesome item about the narratives is in regard to location. For biblical scholars who do not take the Gospel Texts at face value, there is wide debate regarding the location of Jesus' birth. While both Matthew and Luke state that Jesus was born in Bethlehem, scholars working from a scientific and historical

---

[1] Matthew and Luke both held different writing styles and foci. Their goals in writing helped to shape the Text so it's best to let them stay separate. David Neale writes specifically about the contrast in the infancy narratives in Matthew and Luke: "The difference in tone and substance is striking…Luke's political lens is global, emphasizing the birth in 'the entire Roman world,' while Matthew's is distinctively local, focusing on Herod, the client king of Palestine." David A. Neale, *Luke 1-9: A Commentary in the Wesleyan Tradition* (Kansas City: Beacon Hill Press, 2011), 75.

perspective argue against that likelihood. Part of this doubt stems from the "trouble" of the infancy narratives themselves. Without wanting to jump into the murky lake of scholarly approaches to textual traditions, manuscripts, inspiration and the like, let's take a small step into a muddy puddle and consider the difference between the accounts of Jesus' birth and infancy with that of the rest of His life. Scholar Raymond Brown, in his very thorough commentary on the birth of Jesus, writes that "the infancy material has an origin and a historical quality quite different from that of the rest of the Gospels..."[2] Indeed, many scholars believe the infancy narratives to have been written last and are thus the youngest of the narratives that entered into the Gospels of Luke and Matthew. The accounts of Jesus and His ministry were widely viewed and could easily have been transmitted earlier, but regarding the infancy narratives, well, there weren't many witnesses. Think about it-who was there at Jesus' birth? Mary, Joseph, and Jesus. Since the disciples were not there to witness Jesus' birth and give account for it, its historical transmission likely has a different path.[3] Because of this, critical scholars consider all the outside evidence to determine where Jesus was born rather than simply accept His birthplace as Bethlehem. Raymond Brown concedes that the evidence for Jesus' birth in Bethlehem is less than the evidence of Jesus belonging to the lineage of King David.[4] James Charlesworth, in his book entitled *The Historical Jesus*, supplies six different sites as the birthplace of Jesus, while stating that the majority of historians view Nazareth as the most likely.[5]

While believers can admit that there are a lot of uncertainties and unknowns regarding the infancy narratives, that does not mean that we ought to question every single detail or view the narratives as untrue. The Gospels are history, but they are history written to convey the story of Jesus the Messiah-the Savior of the world. The Text we have has been passed down to us and is understood as inspired

---

[2] Raymond E. Brown, *Birth of the Messiah; a New Updated Edition - A Commentary on the Infancy Narratives in the Gospels of Matthew and Luke* (Yale University Press, 1999), 6.

[3] James H. Charlesworth, *The Historical Jesus: An Essential Guide* (Nashville, TN: Abingdon Press, 2008), 70.

[4] Brown, *Birth of the Messiah*, 513.

[5] Charlesworth, *The Historical Jesus*, 71-74.

and authoritative. Even if there are uncertainties, I am content with accepting Jesus' birthplace as Bethlehem as the Gospels suggest.

Reverting back to the difficulty of location…working with the understanding as the Text says that Jesus was born in the city of Bethlehem, where *specifically* in the city was He born? Was He born in a stable as the Nativity scene typically shows? Was he born in a cave? Was he born in someone's house or an Airbnb? The only Scripture Text that addresses the specific locale for Jesus' birth is Luke 2:7: "She wrapped him in cloths and placed him in a manger, because there was no guest room available for them." The reader automatically thinks a stable because Jesus was laid in a manger. Yet, it is possible he was born in a building or a cave. All we know is that because of unfavorable conditions he was laid down in a manger (Mary had to take a short break, ya know?).

We may also wonder about the specific location of Jesus and Mary when the Magi visit. As we have seen, it is difficult to pinpoint with any certainty exactly when and where the magi visited Jesus. While Matthew chapter 2 leads the reader to believe Jesus and His family are in Bethlehem, some critical scholars debate this locale, arguing for Nazareth. I don't support that view at all. King Herod sends the magi to Bethlehem, and afterward responds with the massacre of the innocents in and around Bethlehem. No specific mention of Nazareth occurs until the family returns from Egypt.

One clue we have as to the setting in the Text is in Matthew 2:11 when the magi visit Jesus at the house. The Greek word for house is οἶκος/oikos (yes, like the yogurt brand). It means house/home/dwelling when used in a literal/concrete sense. Its ambiguity does not give us much direction as to the exact locale of where Jesus was when the magi visited: a standard house, stable, a cave? It seems to me that a temporary cave or a stable being used for shelter would not be labeled as οἶκος in the Text. This fact seems to push against the common "Nativity scene" where the magi visit the Christ child in a stable surrounded by animals. Nevertheless, we are still left with some uncertainty as to what sort of place the holy family was when the magi visited. Was it their house/home, or someone else's?

All things considered, there is a lot of uncertainty regarding the infancy narratives especially in regard to chronology and location. It is best to take Matthew and Luke as separate and not try to mash them together. Each author had their own specific way of presenting the story of Jesus. We ought to receive it as we have been given, even if it is without all the details.

ACKNOWLEDGEMENTS

First and foremost, I would like to thank my Lord and Savior Jesus Christ for His unending mercy and grace. I thank Him for putting this book into my mind and heart.

A special thanks to my wife, Edith, for her love and support through all of my research, rambling, and writing. You are my favorite geek. Thanks for putting up with me.

My sons: M, L, and K. You three provided a lot of great inspiration and content for the book. Without you, this book would have been published sooner but would not have been nearly as good. 😊

I extend my gratitude to my wonderful editor, G.S. I deeply appreciate your proofreading, support, and kind words on my manuscript.

I hold great respect for my former pastors and professors. You helped instill a love for God's Word in my life and gave me a lot of wisdom for the road ahead.

Last of all, I thank all who have decided to read this book. Keep on reading and studying God's Word.

BIBLIOGRAPHY

Allison, Gregg R. *The Baker Compact Dictionary of Theological Terms.* *EBSCOhost.* Grand Rapids, MI: Baker Books, 2016.

Aquinas, Thomas. *Catena Aurea: Commentary on the Four Gospels.* Translated by John Henry Newman. Vol. 1. London: J.G.F. and J. Rivington, 1841.

"Audio: BBC Mars Anniversary of KJV Bible with Gay Slur." The Christian Institute, January 17, 2011. https://www.christian.org.uk/news/audio-bbc-mars-400th-anniversary-of-kjv-bible-with-gay-slur/.

Augustine. *Sermons on the Liturgical Seasons: (184-229Z).* Edited by John E. Rotelle. Translated by Edmund Hill. Vol. 6. Brooklyn, N.Y: New City Press, 1993.

Barclay, William. *The Gospel of Matthew.* Vol. 1. Philadelphia: Westminster Press, 1975.

Barclay, William. *The Letters to the Philippians, Colossians, and Thessalonians.* Philadelphia: Westminster Press, 1975.

Barnstone, Willis. *The Other Bible: Jewish Pseudepigrapha, Christian Apocrypha, Gnostic Scriptures, Kabbalah, Dead Sea Scrolls.* San Francisco etc.: HarperSanFrancisco, 1984.

Barton, John. *The Word: How we Translate the Bible-and Why it Matters.* New York: Basic Books, 2023.

Berlin, Naphtali Tzvi Yehuda. "Haamek Sheilah on Sheiltot d'rav Achai Gaon, Kidmat Haemek, Part III 5:7." Translated by Elchanan Greenman. Sefaria. Accessed April 3, 2025. https://www.sefaria.org/Haamek_Sheilah_on_Sheiltot_d'Rav_Achai_Gaon?tab=contents

Box, G. H., and J Landsman, eds. *The Apocalypse of Abraham*. 2nd ed. New York: MacMillan, 1919.

Brown, Raymond E. *Birth of the Messiah; a New Updated Edition - A Commentary on the Infancy Narratives in the Gospels of Matthew and Luke*. Yale University Press, 1999.

Budge, E. A. Wallis. *The Book of the Cave of Treasures: A History of the Patriarchs and the Kings, their Successors, from the Creation to the Crucifixion of Christ, Translated from the Syriac Text of the British Museum Ms. Add. 25875*. London: Religious Tract Society, 1927.

Carroll, Lewis, and John Tenniel. *Through the Looking-Glass, and What Alice Found There*. Philadelphia: Henry Altemus, 1897.

Charles, Robert Henry, ed. *The Apocrypha and Pseudepigrapha of the Old Testament. 1, Apocrypha*. Oxford: Clarendon press, 1983.

Charlesworth, James H. *The Historical Jesus: An Essential Guide*. Nashville, TN: Abingdon Press, 2008.

Charlesworth, James. "Serpent." In *T & T Clark Encyclopedia of Second Temple Judaism* 2, edited by Daniel M. Gurtner, 2:726–27. London: T & T Clark, 2020.

Church of the Nazarene Manual 2023. Kansas City: The Foundry Publishing, 2024.

Coker, William. "Type, Typology." Essay. In *Beacon Dictionary of Theology*, edited by J. Kenneth Grider, Willard H. Taylor, and Richard S Taylor, 532–33. Kansas City, Mo: Beacon Hill Press of Kansas City, 1983.

Coxe, A. Cleveland, and Irenaeus. *Ante-Nicene Fathers: The Writings of the Fathers Down to A.D. 325*. Edited by Alexander Roberts and James Donaldson. Vol. 1. Peabody: Hendrickson, 1995.

Dickerson, Matthew. "Who Gets Left Behind?" *Christianity Today*, June 2011.

Didymus the Blind. *Fathers of the Church: a New Translation. Commentary on Genesis*. Translated by Robert Hill. Catholic University of America Press, 2016.

Eckenstein, Lina. *Comparative Studies in Nursery Rhymes*. London: Duckworth & Co., 1906.

Elliott, James Keith. *A Synopsis of the Apocryphal Nativity and Infancy Narratives*. Leiden: Brill, 2016.

Elwell, Walter A., and Philip Wesley Comfort, eds. *Tyndale Bible Dictionary*. Wheaton, Ill: Tyndale House Publishers, 2001.

Enns, Pete, and John Levison. "Episode 269: Jack Levison - The Greek Life of Adam & Eve." The Bible For Normal People, April 22, 2024. https://thebiblefornormalpeople.com/episode-269-jack-levison-the-greek-life-of-adam-eve/.

Gigot, Francis. "Scriptural Glosses." Catholic Encyclopedia. Accessed November 5, 2025. https://www.newadvent.org/cathen/06586a.htm#section5.

Goldingay, John. *Isaiah. EBSCOhost*. Grand Rapids, Mich: Baker Books, 2012.

Green, Joel B., and Richard B. Hays. "The Use of the Old Testament by New Testament Writers." Essay. In *Hearing the New Testament: Strategies for Interpretation*, edited by Joel B. Green, 122–39. Grand Rapids, Mich: W.B. Eerdmans Pub. Co, 2010.

Grenz, Stanley J. *The Millennial Maze: Sorting Out Evangelical Options*. Downers Grove, Ill: InterVarsity Press, 1992.

Grypeou, Emmanouela, and Helen Spurling. *The Book of Genesis in Late Antiquity: Encounters between Jewish and Christian Exegesis*. Leiden: Brill, 2013.

Harding, James E. *The Love of David and Jonathan: Ideology, Text, Reception*. London: Routledge, Taylor & Francis Group, 2013.

Heacock, Anthony. "Wrongly Framed? The 'David and Jonathan Narrative' and the Writing of Biblical Homosexuality [Sic]." *The Bible and Critical Theory* 3, no. 2 (2007): 22.1-22.14. https://doi.org/10.2104/bc070022.

Hein, Timothy P. "The First Christian 'Magicians': Early Christian Afterlives of Matthew's Magi (Matt 2:1-12)." Thesis, University of Edinburgh, 2021.

"How the Forbidden Fruit Became an Apple." Rutgers University, February 26, 2023. https://www.rutgers.edu/news/how-forbidden-fruit-became-apple.

Hultberg, Alan, Craig A. Blaising, and Douglas J. Moo. *Three Views on the Rapture: Pretribulation, Prewrath, or Posttribulation.* 2nd ed. Grand Rapids, Mich: Zondervan, 2010.

"Humpty Dumpty." The ABC of It: Why Children's Books Matter. Accessed November 20, 2024. https://gallery.lib.umn.edu/exhibits/show/abc-of-it--why-children-s-book/pop-culture/humpty-dumpty.

"Humpty Dumpty Was Code For..." History Daily, October 27, 2022. https://historydaily.org/what-humpty-dumpty-really-means/3.

Hurlbut, Jesse Lyman. *Hurlbut's Life of Christ For Young and Old.* Philadelphia, PA: The John C. Winston Company, 1915.

"Jewish Concepts: Satan." Jewish Virtual Library, 2024. https://www.jewishvirtuallibrary.org/satan.

Kaplan, Paul H. D. *The Rise of the Black Magus in Western Art.* Ann Arbor, Mich: UMI Research Press, 1985.

Kennedy, Titus M. *Excavating the Evidence for Jesus: The Archaeology and History of Christ and the Gospels.* Eugene, OR: Harvest House Publishers, 2022.

Koester, Craig R. *Revelation and the End of All Things.* 2nd ed. Grand Rapids, MI: William B. Eerdmans Publishing Company, 2018.

Levison, John R. *The Greek Life of Adam and Eve.* Berlin: De Gruyter, 2023.

Loew , Judah. "Derekh Chayyim 5:17:7." Translated by R. Francis Nataf. Sefaria. Accessed April 3, 2025. https://www.sefaria.org/Derekh_Chayyim.5.17.7?ven=english%7CSefaria_Edition_2021_by_R._Francis_Nataf&lang=en&with=About&lang2=en.

Lyons, George. "Premillennialism." Essay. In *Beacon Dictionary of Theology*, edited by Richard S. Taylor, J. Kenneth Grider, and Willard H. Taylor, 414. Kansas City, Mo: Beacon Hill Press of Kansas City, 1983.

McGrath, Alister E. *Christian Theology: An Introduction*. 4th ed. Malden: Blackwell Publ, 2007.

Merkle, Benjamin L. "Who Will Be Left Behind? Rethinking the Meaning of Matthew 24:40-41 and Luke 17:34-35." *Westminster Theological Journal* 72 (2010): 169–79.

Morris, J B, and Edward Johnston, trans. "Hymns on the Nativity." Church Fathers: Hymns on the Nativity (Ephraim), 2023. https://www.newadvent.org/fathers/3703.htm.

My Jewish Learning. "Do Jews Believe in Satan?" My Jewish Learning, 2022. https://www.myjewishlearning.com/article/satan-the-adversary/.

Neale, David A. *Luke 1-9: A Commentary in the Wesleyan Tradition*. Kansas City: Beacon Hill Press, 2011.

"No Conversion for Tavern Tunes." The Washington Times, August 21, 2002. https://www.washingtontimes.com/news/2002/aug/21/20020821-041030-4581r/.

Oden, Thomas C., and Andrew Louth, eds. *Ancient Christian Commentary on Scripture. Old Testament: Vol. 1: Genesis 1-11*. Vol. 1. Downers Grove, IL: InterVarsity Press, 2001.

OJ, Lakhani, and Lakhani JD. "Endocrinology and 'Humpty Dumpty.'" *Indian Journal of Endocrinology and Metabolism* 24 (October 19, 2020): 509–11.

Oswalt, John N. *Isaiah*. Grand Rapids, MI: Zondervan Academic, 2010.

Paulas, Rick. "What Happened to Doomsday Prophet Harold Camping after the World Didn't End?" Vice, July 29, 2024. https://www.vice.com/en/article/life-after-doomsday-456/.

Phillips, Elaine A. "Serpent Intertexts: Tantalizing Twists in the Tales." *Bulletin for Biblical Research* 10, no. 2 (2000): 233–45.

Phillips, Rob. "Humpty Dumpty the Cannon, Not the Egg…" Fisher Jones Greenwood Solicitors, February 27, 2015. https://www.fjg.co.uk/blog/humpty-dumpty-cannon-not-egg.

Powell, Mark Allan. *Matthew: An Interpretation Bible Commentary*. Louisville, KY: Westminster John Knox Press, 2023.

Powell, Mark Allan. "The Magi as Kings: An Adventure in Reader-Response Criticism." *The Catholic Biblical Quarterly* 62, no. 3 (2000): 459–80.

Presley, Stephen O. *The Intertextual Reception of Genesis 1-3 in Irenaeus of Lyons*. Leiden: Brill, 2015.

Rappoport, Jason, ed. "Bereshit Rabbah." Translated by Joshua Schreier. Sefaria. Accessed November 12, 2023. https://www.sefaria.org/Bereshit_Rabbah.

Robinson, Bernard. "Matthew's Nativity Stories: Historical and Theological Questions for Today's Readers." Essay. In *New Perspectives on the Nativity*, edited by Jeremy Corley, 110–31. New York, NY: T & T Clark International, 2009.

Ryrie, Charles Caldwell. *The Ryrie Study Bible: New American Standard Translation: With Introductions, Annotations, Outlines, Marginal References, Harmony of the Gospels, Synopsis of Bible Doctrine, Index of Scripture, Index to Notes, Concordance, Maps, and Timeline Charts and Many Other Helps*. Chicago: Moody Press, 1978.

Schofield, Philip. "Jeremy Bentham: Prophet of Secularism." Journal of Bentham Studies, September 17, 2024. https://journals.uclpress.co.uk/jbs/article/id/3260/.

Schowalter, Daniel N. "Magi." Essay. In *The Oxford Guide to People & Places of the Bible*, edited by Michael David Coogan and Bruce Manning Metzger, 187–88. Oxford: Oxford Univ. Press, 2004.

Simonetti, Manlio, and Thomas C. Oden, eds. *Ancient Christian commentary on Scripture: New Testament. 1A, Matthew 1-13*. Downers Grove, Ill: InterVarsity Press, 2001.

Stitzinger, James F. "The Rapture in Twenty Centuries of Biblical Interpretation." *The Master's Seminary Journal* 13, no. 2 (2002): 149–71.

Strong, James. *The New Strong's Exhaustive Concordance of the Bible: With Main Concordance, Appendix to the Main Concordance, Topical Index to the Bible, Dictionary of the Hebrew Bible, Dictionary of the Greek Testament*. Nashville: T. Nelson Publishers, 1984.

Telushkin, Joseph. *Biblical Literacy: The Most Important People, Events, and Ideas of the Hebrew Bible*. New York: HarperCollins, 2002.

Terian, Abraham, trans. *The Armenian Gospel of the Infancy: With Three Early Versions of the Protoevangelium of James*. Oxford: Oxford University Press, 2008.

Thaumaturgus, Gregory. *Ante-Nicene fathers: The Writings of the Fathers down to A.D. 325*. Edited by Alexander Roberts and James Donaldson. Vol. 6. Peabody: Hendrickson, 1995.

Vanden Eykel, Eric. *The Magi: Who they were, How they've been Remembered, and Why they still Fascinate*. Minneapolis, MN: Fortress Press, 2022.

Verrett, Brian A. *The Serpent in Samuel: A Messianic Motif*. Eugene, OR: Resource Publications, 2020.

Wesley, John. "Wesley Center Online." The Wesley Center Online: John Wesley's Notes on the Bible. Accessed June 5, 2025. https://wesley.nnu.edu/john-wesley/john-wesleys-notes-on-the-bible/.

Wright, N. T. *Surprised by Hope*. New York: HarperOne, 2018.

Zehnder, Markus. "Observations on the Relationship between David and Jonathan and the Debate on Homosexuality." *The Westminster Theological Journal* 69, no. 1 (2007): 127–74.

Zevit, Ziony. *What Really Happened in the Garden of Eden?* New Haven: Yale University Press, 2013.

FINAL NOTES

———— • ————

Ω AI was not used in the writing of the manuscript of this book.

Ω Images in this book come from a variety of sources. With the exception of the cover image, all images are either public domain or furnished by the author. Some images were created by the author using AI with specific prompts.

Ω I do not give permission for this book to be used for the training and development of AI engines.

Ω I do not give permission for this book to be used by extraterrestrials for learning English or human customs. They do have permission to observe and enjoy the images in the book.

Ω If my brother does not read this (as proof of reading my entire book), he owes me a round of golf this summer.

9 798994 995501